BASIC
Mountain Safety

FROM A TO Z

by

J. Leslie Johnson

Altitude Publishing
The Canadian Rockies / British Columbia / Colorado

PUBLICATION INFORMATION

Altitude Publishing Canada Ltd.

The Canadian Rockies / British Columbia / Colorado
Head Office: 1500 Railway Avenue
Canmore, Alberta T1W 1P6

Copyright 2000 © J. Leslie Johnson

Cataloging in Publication Data

Johnson, Joan Leslie
Basic mountain safety
Includes index.
ISBN 1-55265-023-5
1. Mountaineering--Safety measures. I. Title.
GV200.18.J64 2000 796.52'2'0289 C99 911290 2

Printed and bound in Western Canada by Friesens, Altona, Manitoba.

Altitude GreenTree Program

Altitude Publishing will plant twice as many trees as were used in the manufacturing of this product.

We acknowledge the financial support of the Government of Canada through the Book Publishing Industry Development Program (BPIDP) for our publishing activities.

Photographs

Front Cover: Rocky Mountain National Park
Back Cover: Rocky Mountain National Park

Dedication

This book is dedicated to Klarns Johnson

Project Development

Publisher	Stephen Hutchings
Associate Publishers	Dan Klinglesmith
	Patrick Soran
Concept/Art Direction	Stephen Hutchings
Design/Layout	Dan Klinglesmith
Editor	Dan Klinglesmith
Illustrations	Kitty McLeod
Index	Elizabeth Bell
Financial Management	Laurie Smith

A Note from the Publisher

The world described in *Altitude SuperGuides* is a unique and fascinating place. It is a world filled with surprise and discovery, beauty and enjoyment, questions and answers. It is a world of people, cities, landscape, animals and wilderness as seen through the eyes of those who live in, work with, and care for this world. The process of describing this world is also a means of defining ourselves.

It is also a world of relationship, where people derive their meaning from a deep and abiding contact with the land—as well as from each other. And it is this sense of relationship that guides all of us at Altitude to ensure that these places continue to survive and evolve in the decades ahead.

Altitude SuperGuides are books intended to be used, as much as read. Like the world they describe, Altitude SuperGuides are evolving, adapting and growing. Please write to us with your comments and observations, and we will do our best to incorporate your ideas into future editions of these books.

Stephen Hutchings
Publisher

CONTENTS

THE BASICS

Most accidents in the mountains can be prevented with some knowledge. If people can identify potential objective hazards, they can learn how to avoid them. This can be accomplished through routefinding, choosing a different excursion or route, or simply turning back. Mountains pose dangers but are not always dangerous. At the same time, mountains offer people an unparalleled opportunity to enjoy the exquisite beauty of Nature, to relax, seek solitude, or get exercise. This book identifies some of the basic objective hazards that exist in the Rocky Mountains and the overall purpose is prevention. The book can be summed up quite simply: See the hazard, avoid the hazard, prevent the accident. Your knowledge—of the mountains and of your own abilities—is your best equipment for enjoying the mountains safely.

Before going to the mountains however, experts recommend that you take some time to plan your trip. For example, Canadian mountain rescue specialist Lloyd Gallagher says that many unfortunate incidents in the mountains could be prevented with proper planning. "Although I have been venturing into the mountains for decades, I still refer to my checklist to make sure I have the equipment, first aid and other essentials I need," Gallagher explains. "Otherwise, it is easy to forget an item which can become very important when in the mountains." The steps listed below are broadly based on the extensive mountain experience which he has gained over the years. Use them as a basic checklist to plan your mountain adventures.

"The mountaineer returns to his hills because he remembers always that he has forgotten so much."

—Goeffrey Winthrop Young

1. RESEARCH THE ROUTE: Before embarking on the trip, study the route to see if it is within your abilities. You can obtain information about the route from people who have already done it, knowledgeable people such as park rangers and wardens, and from trip reports and guidebooks.

Why People Get Into Trouble in the Mountains

Lloyd "Kiwi" Gallagher

Lloyd Gallagher, an accomplished mountain climber, deputy leader of the first Canadian expedition to climb Mount Everest,

and former manager of the Public Safety Program at Kananaskis Park in Alberta, Canada, has several decades of experience in mountain search and rescue.

Why do people get into trouble in the mountains? Gallagher says mountain adventurers simply do not recognize the messages that Nature is giving them.

"In the city, we have signal lights which turn from green to orange to red," explains Gallagher. "Green means go ahead, orange means exercise caution, and red means stop."

The search and rescue specialist believes Nature also provides signals which are as obvious as the green, orange, and red lights in the city. "You would not run a red light in the city, so why would you do so in the mountains?" asks the mountain guide. "Only one thing will happen: You will be stopped."

Gallagher believes that people can learn to recognize Nature's warning signals. And if they obey the red lights, people can maintain their safety and maximize their enjoyment of this magnificent environment.

Left: Learning about objective and subjective hazards increases the safety margin in the mountains.

2. FIND OUT ABOUT HAZARDS THAT ARE ESPECIALLY PREVALENT IN THE AREA:
For example, loose rock is not a significant hazard when hiking or climbing the granite domes and peaks found in Yosemite National Park, California. However, in Banff National Park, Alberta, loose rock is a major hazard because much of the rock consists of easily fractured limestone. Many scrambling or climbing accidents occur near Banff because visitors from other countries are not aware of the fragile nature of the rock.

If you are uncertain of your abilities or the difficulty of the route, you might consider going with more experienced people, joining a hiking or skiing club, or taking courses in aspects such as navigation, first aid or mountaineering. After making your first choice of a route, select an alternative in

Subjective Hazards

Subjective factors are aspects brought to the mountains such as fitness.

An interview with Geoff Powter, mountaineer, psychologist, and editor of the *Canadian Alpine Journal.*

What are "subjective hazards?" Do they play a role in mountain accidents?

GP: Subjective factors are the things you bring into the mountains. They include awareness of your own limitations, your motivational state, your fitness level, and your psychological preparedness for the outdoor adventure. Most of the research on risk assessment shows problems often occur as a result of people getting into situations they could have avoided.

How might outdoor adventurers deal with the subjective factor?

GP: It is important to understand that your psychology, motivation, and mentality have a strong influence on what you do. And so it is important to be curious about why you think or act the way you do when you are doing outdoor sports. Objective hazards—such as poor rock quality and avalanche danger—are always present in the mountains. And you need to have an understanding of them. But if you do not master yourself, you will likely have a hard time applying whatever knowledge you have to the situation or controlling it.

Does greater self-awareness encourage people to take greater risks in the outdoors?

GP: Many people were initially risk takers when they got into outdoor sports. Over time, they have come to understand there is a kind of excitement in managing the risk. Ultimately, that is what we want to do: We do not take risks for the sake of entering ourselves into danger. We take risks to have the experience and master those risks or perceive we master those risks. That is the psychological kernel of the experience as far as I am concerned; the "flow experience" is what we look for in outdoor sports more than anything else.

What is the "flow experience"?

GP: The flow experience is a term used to describe what people are looking for in any kind of "peak" experience. It identifies the state of mind you can get into when you challenge yourself and you find a perfect mix of the task and your own abilities in that challenge. They come together so you get a mindfulness of what you are doing; you slip into a state in which you are perfectly in tune with the task ahead of you.

Success in the Mountains: What is It?

Jamie Clarke

An interview with Jamie Clarke, adventurer, mountaineer, and explorer who ascended the summit of Mount Everest in 1997 and then later went on to cross the Empty Quarter of the Arabian Desert.

Your team did not make the summit of Everest on its first two attempts. Do you see this as a "failure" or a "success?"

JC: In the beginning, as an athlete and as a climber, everything was about reaching the summit. Almost any manner of sacrifice would be put forth to realize that outcome. But through those years, between the first and sec-

ond climbs, I began to realize that ultimately the summit was not the end but the means—the excuse, the vision, the beacon on the horizon—that I could shoot for. The summit was just a sexy reason or an excuse to go off and have a grand adventure and learn much.

You made the summit on your third attempt. Did this trip feel more like a "success" than the first two?

JC: In my heart, I believe the day I made the summit was one of those special days, one of a handful of days for which I was truly born. It was a magical trip

for me, and I think about it often. But when I came home, it wasn't an amazingly contrasting experience from my other adventures, which I thought were filled with victory as well. The flavor of the victory was different but the essence was the same: You set the goal, you trained for it, you learned along the way, you struggled with friendships, you fought, you argued, you beat back your fears and your doubts and your questions, and you went on and climbed and climbed and climbed.

What advice would you give to others who feel the need to "make the summit" in order to achieve "success"?

JC: My advice would be to give yourself permission to fail. That is probably the greatest gift I have ever given myself—permission to fail. And it sounds weird to say that because we have almost a stigma about failure—we feel that it is a bad thing. But I believe failure is the greatest teacher available to us in life. And I believe that the mountains are a wonderful place and that they should be accessible to everyone. Reaching the summit—any summit—is ultimately irrelevant and basically unimportant compared to the experiences you have on your way.

Basic Clothing Checklist

While every person who ventures into the high country needs to customize their own clothing needs to meet their individual requirements, at the minimum consider the following items:

❏ **Inner layer:** Underwear tops and pants. In cold weather, add a second layer or a heavier layer.

❏ **Middle layer:** Tops and pants to add warmth. In cold weather, add a heavier weight vest or jacket.

❏ **Outer layer:** Pants and jacket that are wind resistant, water resistant and breathable. In cold weather add heavier weight jacket.

❏ **Rain gear:** Coated nylon or waterproof/breathable pants and jacket.

❏ **Head gear:** Hat for warmth, balaclava or facemask to protect your face from cold and wind; a hood for wind protection; a light cap or hat for sun protection.

❏ **Hands:** Light inner layer, wind resistant, water-resistant over-mitts.

❏ **Socks:** Light inner layer. In cold weather, add heavier outer layer.

❏ **Footwear:** Comfortable hiking boots, mountaineering boots or ski boots. Neoprene booties for river crossings, light sandals for sore feet, down booties for cold feet, gaiters to keep your legs dry and your feet warm.

Note: In cold or wet weather, do not use cotton. Instead, use various synthetic fabrics to wick away moisture.

Basic Gear Checklist

The planned activity will influence the gear list, but always consider the following for any outing:

❏ **Food and water:** Lunch, extra food, snacks, water bottle, thermos. Electrolyte replacement for hot weather or prolonged, strenuous exercise.

❏ **Headlamp:** Flashlight or headlamp, extra batteries and bulb

❏ **Navigation equipment:** Map, compass, whistle; optional altimeter and /or GPS

❏ **Sun protection:** Sunscreen (SPF 15 or higher), lip protection, and sunglasses with side flaps, or goggles

❏ **Fire starting equipment:** Matches and/or lighter, firestarter, and/ or candle

❏ **Emergency shelter:** Bivouac bag, space blanket, and/or heavy garbage bags

❏ **Repair kit:** For bike, skis, ski bindings, snowshoes, and pack. Pocket knife as survival tool

❏ **Insulation:** Foam pad or inflatable pad for overnight trips

❏ **Walking stick:** Hiking or ski poles; walking stick or ice ax

❏ **Umbrella** (optional)**:** For hiking and camping in the rain; for sun protection

❏ **Insect repellent:** Containing DEET or other effective repellent

❏ **Water purifier:** Chemical or filter or combination

❏ **Camera** (optional)**:** Camera, film, and batteries

❏ **Book** (optional)**:** For those long rainy days inside the tent or overnight trips

Basic Footcare

Make sure your footwear fits properly before venturing into the mountains.

Blisters are caused by friction: The skin rubs against another object and a small tear forms on the epidermis (the outer layer of the skin) while also filling with fluid. Although a blister is a minor injury, it can turn a pleasurable hike or ski trip into a slog. A blister can also lead to infections and bleeding. Taking care of your feet goes a long way to ensuring your comfort in the backcountry.

What are some of the major causes of blisters? Boots that are too large or too small can cause blisters, as can socks that are wrinkled or have holes in them. If the boot is too loose, the foot can slide forward and cause "downhill blisters" to form on the toes or front of the foot. In contrast, "uphill blisters" form on the heel of the foot.

How can you prevent blisters? Make sure your boots fit properly before venturing into the mountains. If the boots are made of a rugged material such as hardy

leather, break them in slowly before wearing them on long trips. Some experts recommend wearing two pair of socks: a thick outer pair and a thinner inner pair. By doing this, the socks rub against each other, instead of against your skin. Other people recommend applying a generous amount of lubricant such as petroleum jelly over the entire foot. This again prevents the friction that can cause blisters. Conversely, you can apply powder to your foot. This helps prevent your skin from clinging to your boot. Or, you can tape areas that are susceptible to blisters before embarking on your trip.

What can you do if you get a blister? The first rule is to attend to the blister right away. Resist the urge to tough it out, as this will only make the blister worse. As soon as you notice a hot spot, stop and attend to the would-be blister. Make sure you cover reddish areas with tape or moleskin.

If a blister has already formed, protect it from further abrasion by applying a doughnut-shaped piece of moleskin around the blister. Apply tape to keep the moleskin in place and keep pressure off the wound.

What about breaking the blister? Physicians recommend that you do not break the blister because this can result in infection. The wound will heal more quickly and hurt less if the roof of the blister remains. However, if it has already broken, clean the blistered area and cover it with a sterile dressing. And if you absolutely must break a blister, first clean the area using soap and water. Insert a sterile needle at the side of blister to gently open it. Apply gentle pressure to coax the fluid out and then cover the blister with a sterile dressing. And, keep feet clean. This is a further safeguard against possible infection.

THE BASICS
(continued)

case weather, trail conditions or other factors make your first choice inadvisable. You also need to make reservations or obtain trail permits before going into certain busy or ecologically sensitive areas.

3. OBTAIN A TOPOGRAPHIC MAP OF THE AREA: Check whether it is up-to-date by asking knowledgeable people. Otherwise, you might plan your trip based on a topographical feature such as bridge or road only to discover when you actually get there that this key aspect of your route no longer exists.

4. OBTAIN THE EQUIPMENT AND GEAR YOU NEED: After deciding upon your route, and getting up-to-date information about its possible hazards, make a list of the equipment and gear you will need. Having adequate equipment and clothing is a vital aspect of mountain safety. For example, light running shoes do not provide adequate support in mountain terrain such as boulder fields or snow-covered scree. Inadequate equipment leads to minor incidents such as a twisted ankle or major accidents such as a broken leg.

"Late starts are a common problem."

Lloyd Gallagher

Follow the principle of layering when choosing your clothes. Layering enables you to regulate your temperature: when you get too hot, you take off a layer. When you get too cold, you add a layer. Layering works because of dead air. When you exercise, you generate heat and warm up the dead air trapped between your clothing. The dead air provides an effective layer of insulation.

Basic First Aid Checklist

These basic first aid items are essential requirements for anyone venturing into the mountains, even for short outings.

❏ **Moderate cuts and scrapes:** Adhesive tape, roller gauze, triangular bandages, gauze

❏ **Removing embedded items:** Scissors, tweezers

❏ **Major cuts and injuries:** Assorted sterile dressings, safety pins, duct tape

❏ **Minor injuries such as blisters:** Dressing such as moleskin

❏ **Pain relief:** Over the counter pain relievers, anti-inflammatory, personal medications

❏ **Reference and recording:** First aid manual, accident report, pencil, emergency telephone numbers

Basic Survival Kit Checklist

Many mountain experts advise making up your own survival kit rather than buying a pre-packaged one in a store. This enables you to personalize the kit according to your own needs and the objective hazards of the area you plan to explore.

One mountain adventurer, Len Bradley, after completing a series of wilderness travel courses, devised his own kit.

The small tin kit fits into the palm of his hand and is easy to carry. His personal survival kit contains the following:

❏ **First Aid:** Large dressing, Band-Aids, painkiller, steel needle

❏ **Fire:** Waterproof matches and striker, birthday candles and waxed string to start a fire

❏ **Signal:** Whistle, lid of tin for mirror, cards and pencil for notes

❏ **Navigation:** Small compass

❏ **Food:** Packet of instant cereal, envelope of sugar, candy, tea bag, salt, snare wire, hooks and fishing line

❏ **Miscellaneous:** Small knife, razor blade, string, tape

CHECKING YOUR ROUTE

1. THE TRAIL

Is the current path the easiest way to reach your destination? Is there any reason why you should not proceed along this route such as trail closures due to bears or other hazards? Do you have adequate equipment and food and water?

2. YOUR PROGRESS

How far have you traveled along your route? Do you have enough time to make your objective and return comfortably? Might you end up spending a night out if you continue?

3. ROUTE DIFFICULTY

Is it harder or easier than you anticipated? Is the trip longer than you thought? Are you feeling strong or tired? How long will it take you to get back?

4. THE CONDITIONS

Consider the weather and trail conditions as your trip unfolds. Consider again your strength and equipment. Do not hesitate to turn back if factors such as weather suggest it would be wise to retreat.

Mountain weather is unpredictable and can change quickly. It can vary from valley to valley and from valley to ridge. Hazards such as avalanches and rockfall may occur due to sudden temperature extremes. Weather can change the difficulty of your route. Get a current weather forecast before you start your trip and plan accordingly. Watch the weather as you go.

1. It is generally colder and windier on peaks and ridges than valley bottoms. Put on a windproof layer or have your lunch before reaching ridges. Take shelter in natural windbreaks such as trees and boulders. Travel along trees or valley bottoms to decrease wind impact.

2. Clouds may turn into fog at higher altitudes making visibility difficult. Whiteouts can occur over snowfields and glaciers. Bring a map and compass to help you navigate.

3. It can snow or rain at any time of the year in many mountainous areas. Getting wet causes heat to be lost quickly. Bring appropriate rain gear including waterproof or breathable clothing and footgear. Use a waterproof cover to protect your pack.

4. The formation of clouds can herald an approaching thunderstorm. Bring extra clothing and rain gear. Find areas of safety in case of lightning. Descend from ridges. Avoid tall solitary trees, open alpine meadows and lakes. Seek heavy forest, buildings or vehicles, or crouch on your pack.

5. Extremes of hot and cold can occur on the same day. Bring clothing and equipment for both extremes. A warm hat prevents loss of heat from your head in cold conditions. A light hat protects you from the sun's rays. Consider temperature extremes when planning your trip. Carry adequate fluids.

The inner layer—your underwear—provides warmth and wicks moisture away from your body. The middle layer provides you with more insulation. It should also be lightweight and breathable. The outer layer must be sufficient to withstand environmental conditions such as wind, rain, sun, snow and hail. Thus it is useful to have some wind resistant, water resistant or waterproof layers. Garments that are breathable and water-resistant repel water from the outside but reduce condensation on the inside.

You might consider making up a list of clothing and equipment, such as a hat and water bottle, that you would always need when traveling in the mountains. Then, either subtract or add items depending on the requirements of each trip. What you take depends on factors such as your activity, the remoteness of your planned location, the weather, and the experience of your group. Your essential equipment list should also include a repair kit for gear, a first aid kit and a survival kit. Although you can buy many of these in outdoor equipment stores, experts recommend that you make your own kits so you can tailor them to your specific needs.

Backcountry safety experts point out that administering first aid in the mountains is much different than doing so in the city. First of all, time is a factor. While you can obtain help quickly in an urban environment, this is not true of the mountains. It could take minutes in the city but hours or

THE BASICS
(continued)

Summer thunderheads crash ineffectually around the mountaintop like naughty kids buzzing a deaf, dumb, and blind child placidly smiling.

—John Nichols

Basic Firecraft

Being able to make a fire in any season is absolutely essential because its heat will protect you from hypothermia and help warm up your shelter. You can also make two fires and sleep between them. Although you will probably have to get up several times in the night to stoke the fires, they will help keep you warm.

Although you may be able to make a fire using the elements around you, it will be easier if you bring a firestarter. Portable firestarters made of blocks of paraffin wax are available at most outdoor stores. Also bring a lighter and/or waterproof matches.

BASIC STEPS FOR FIRE MAKING:

1. Gather materials for your fire as available. The best option is to collect three types of materials: tinder, kindling and primary fuel.

Tinder is comprised of small pieces of dry vegetation such as bark, dry grass and dead leaves. Kindling is comprised of larger pieces of fuel such as small twigs and dry leaves.

Primary fuel is comprised of larger twigs and branches. When the fire is fully established, primary fuel can include larger items such as logs. Some types of wood do not burn as well as others. For example, woods such as alder and poplar smolder more than they burn while resinous woods such as pine spit.

2. After gathering the materials find a good place to build a fire such as a place sheltered from the wind. If it is winter, the fire will eventually burn through the snow. To prevent this, light the fire on an insulating surface such as a snow shovel, a log or some rocks.

• Stack your larger twigs and branches in a teepee-like shape leaving space at the bottom for your tinder.

3. Insert the tinder inside the teepee and light it. As the tinder catches, carefully add small bits of tinder until it is well lit. Next, add small pieces of twigs and branches to the fire taking care not to add too much too fast.

4. Once the fire establishes itself, the teepee of sticks will fall down and these larger sticks will begin to burn. At this point, continue to add larger sticks.

5. Tend the fire carefully adding more fuel as required. Before leaving the area, make sure the fire is completely extinguished.

days in the mountains. In addition, you can usually provide comfortable shelter in the city—your home or your vehicle, for example. However, in the mountains, shelter can take time to find or build. You may have to construct a makeshift shelter from natural features such as outcrops or materials such as snow or boughs. In the mountains, an accident may not occur in a safe environment. For example, a ridge is a dangerous place to have an accident in an electrical storm. In the mountains, you must be capable of providing first aid to someone who is injured. In the city, you can simply call upon qualified medical personnel for assistance. In addition, you are not required to provide long-term care in an urban environment because it will be available. However, it may be necessary for you to understand the implications for long-term care in the mountains. For example, if poor weather prevents the evacuation of an accident victim, you must continue to care for them.

Basic Map and Compass

Although technological innovations such as the Global Positioning System (GPS) are now available for navigation, search and rescue experts advise that having a basic knowledge of map and compass is essential for travel in mountainous terrain. A topographic map identifies major features such as roads, buildings and waterways. Contour lines on the map indicate terrain features and elevations. Buy a topographic map for the area you plan to visit before embarking on your trip. Check the date of the map to make sure it is current.

A compass has a magnetic needle that is attracted to the magnetic poles of the Earth (north and south). Although many different types of compasses are available, a protractor compass is useful for basic navigation. It makes it possible to take bearings from the map without moving the compass from it. When used together, a map and compass enable you locate your position on a map and determine a direction of travel.

When determining direction, it is useful to know that there are three different norths. While true north is the actual geographic pole, grid north is the north indicated on the map, and magnetic north is the direction to which the compass points. The difference between magnetic north and grid north is called magnetic variation. In some parts of the world, magnetic variation is slight. However, in northern latitudes, the amount of magnetic variation increases. The magnetic variation for a certain area is marked at the foot of most maps. It can be set on a protractor compass.

Before embarking on a mountain adventure, take a bearing using your map and compass. This establishes the angle from point A (the starting point) to point B (the destination) and magnetic north.

1. Place the compass on the map between point A and point B. The direction arrow at the end of the compass should point to point B.

2. Using the scale on the edge of the compass, read the distance between point A and point B. Compare this reading with the scale of the map.

3. Keeping the compass in the same position on the map, turn the central dial until the north-south lines align with the grid lines of the map. The north (red) arrow on the dial of the compass should point to grid north on the map.

4. Keeping the compass in the same position, gently move the map until the north arrow aligns with magnetic north. The needle on the compass indicates this. The direction arrow at the end of the compass now points to the bearing.

To use the compass in the field, hold it level in your hand. Follow the direction arrow. Keep the north arrow on the dial and the magnetic needle in alignment.

Thoughtful planning increases the safety and enjoyment of the high country.

5. CHECK THE WEATHER FORECAST AND TRAIL CONDITIONS: Mountain weather is unpredictable and changes frequently. Weather in the highlands is different from that of the lowlands, and conditions vary from valley to valley. All that said, it is still essential to check the weather before you go because weather can completely change the difficulty of the trip. A forecast of heavy rain could change a three-day backpacking trip into a slog; a heavy snow storm could increase avalanche conditions and make your proposed ski trip too dangerous; extremely high temperatures and no wind could make your hike unwise without carrying extra water.

Trail conditions also change because of last-minute changes in weather. For example, heavy rain the preceding week can make a river too dangerous to cross or turn a trail into a quagmire. Check the trail conditions at park information centers or with other knowledgeable people before you start your trip. If the conditions are not good, either modify the outing or choose another trip.

"Such a peak seldom need exert its strength. For the little insects that challenge its immensities, it sets high the conditions of victory; and it lets them defeat themselves."

—Elizabeth Knowlton

Basic Navigational Devices

GLOBAL POSITIONING SYSTEM (GPS)	ALTIMETER

The Global Positioning System (GPS) makes use of a configuration of 24 satellites that constantly orbit the Earth. A receiver within the GPS reads radio signals that the satellites relay to Earth. Transmitters calculate the positions of about three of the closest satellites. The GPS then provides a fairly precise reading of the location based on the position of the satellites.

Unlike a compass, which indicates direction of travel, an altimeter indicates altitude. Available as a wristwatch or a handheld device, an altimeter is basically a handy barometer. A capsule within the altimeter, called an aneroid box, picks up small shifts in air pressure. The capsule contracts or expands as the air pressure alters and moves a

needle on the altimeter. A dial on the altimeter shows readings in feet or meters. An altimeter helps you locate your position in conditions of low visibility. It is also useful for predicting changes in the weather. The altimeter must be reset regularly against known elevations to compensate for changes in barometric pressure.

THE BASICS
(continued)

6. TELL SOMEONE WHERE YOU ARE GOING: Before you embark on your trip, advise a friend of your proposed trip and alternative routes. Let that person know when you intend to be back, and ask him/her to contact authorities if you do not return on time. Alternatively, leave a note on the dashboard of your vehicle providing this information or register with the appropriate park (if this service is available). If you do this, you may be rescued sooner than if you had not. It also helps rescuers because it narrows the search area.

7. MAKE SURE THAT EVERYONE STAYS TOGETHER. This can be problematic because people walk or ski at different speeds. The fastest person blasts far ahead while the slowest lag far behind. Both may become out of sight of the main group. As you travel, stop periodically to look back over the route; the trail might appear very different when you are coming back. Here are some simple tips you can follow to keep everyone together:

—**KEEP CHILDREN BETWEEN ADULTS:** Children are often playful and energetic, running ahead or off to the side of the trail. They can easily become lost as a result. To avoid this, make sure small children are always between two adults and within sight.

—**GO WITH THE DECISION OF THE MAJORITY:** If you have designated a person to lead the group and make decisions about route finding, follow that person's route. If you are in a group without a designated leader, follow the decision of the majority although you have to sacrifice some of your personal desires.

—**DESIGNATE A "TAIL-END CHARLIE:"** Have a strong person who knows the route tag along behind the slowest member of the group. The strong person makes sure that the weaker person stays on route and does not get lost (or even become disheartened and give up).

"Most of us don't do enough pre-planning. By doing this, we are only setting ourselves at risk."

Lloyd Gallagher

Basic Child Safety Tips

If you take children in the backcountry teach them practical tips about how to avoid getting lost.

• **Stay in sight:** Since children have lots of energy and curiosity, they tend to go off and investigate. Teach them to stay within your sight.

• **Recognize a trail:** For older children teach them the basics of keeping en route. Show them how to recognize a trail and how to interpret trail signs. Give them an easy map to interpret and have them "color" their progress as they proceed. You could also give them a basic compass to play with, and learn from.

• **Ask permission to go somewhere:** If they want to investigate something, even for a short period of time, teach them that they must first obtain your consent.

• **Make noise:** Give your children a whistle and instruct them to blow it if they are in trouble. Emphasize the whistle is not a toy. Tell them to blow it and to make a lot of noise if they need help. This will help other people find them. If you have toddlers who might crawl into the underbrush around your camp, put a bell around their necks. This helps you locate them more easily.

• **Keep warm:** Give the children a small backpack. Put extra clothing, food and a portable shelter such as a large garbage bag in it. Make sure the pack contains a warm hat even in the summer, since people lose substantial heat through the head. Instruct children to put on all of the extra clothing if they become lost. If they are old enough, show them a few places (such as the base of a big tree) where they could find rudimentary natural shelter.

—**WAIT AT TRAIL INTERSECTIONS:** Before proceeding, make sure everyone has caught up. Otherwise, different members of the group make different decisions about what is the "right way to go" and the group becomes separated.

—**ARRANGE A RENDEZVOUS POINT:** Before embarking on your trip, decide where you will meet if members of the group become separated or lost. If your group fails to keep together on the trail, you can at least meet at your designated rendezvous spot. If members of the group do not show up at this place, other members will consider them lost and decide upon an appropriate strategy.

8. CHECK YOUR ROUTE AS YOU GO: Once on your trip, keep an eye out for changing conditions. If weather or other factors make the trip too difficult, turn back and try another route. As you go along, make a note of important landmarks. If conditions change, you may have to retrace your steps and will need to recognize your trail.

Basic Precautions for Going Alone

Traveling alone offers freedom and solitude. It also increases the risk.

Most mountain experts recommend that you go with a group rather than alone. If you are by yourself and get into an accident, no one is available to help you out or go for help. If you tell people where you are going before you leave, and then do not come back on time, rescuers will try to find you. However, remember this takes time. If you are badly hurt that time factor may be critical.

Some mountain adventurers like to go alone because they enjoy solitude. If you do choose to go by yourself, make sure you are completely self-reliant. Pick a route that is well within your abilities. Avoid crossing dangerous areas such as difficult rivers or potential avalanche slopes. Carry extra equipment, food, clothing and a first aid kit. Be able to spend a night or two out if required. Carry a cellular phone or other device such as a signal mirror or flare that will enable you to advise people of your location.

17

ACCIDENT MANAGEMENT

Even the best prepared hikers, campers, or backpackers can face serious accidents. Use the following information to better manage an accident situation.

FIRST STEPS IN TIMES OF CRISIS

• **GET OUT OF IMMEDIATE DANGER:** Since hazards such as an avalanche or rockfall can continue to threaten your party, get everyone out of the way of the hazard. Maintain your own safety when going to the assistance of the person in need. If you blindly rush in, you can become involved in an accident yourself.

• **BE PREPARED TO PROVIDE FIRST AID:** Take courses such as Basic First Aid and Wilderness First Aid. These courses teach how to improvise in a backcountry environment. Based on the knowledge gained, perform urgently needed first aid if required. Remember that providing first aid includes a psychological component. Reassure the victim as needed.

• **EXAMINE THE SITUATION, CONSIDERING FACTORS SUCH AS:**

—Seriousness of any injuries

—Strength of the group

—Weather and temperature

—Difficulty of the terrain

—Remoteness of the location

—Availability of help

—Whether anyone knows where you are and that help might be sent

—Whether anyone can go for help

—Whether there are safe, interim places to stop on the way out

• **MAKE A PLAN AND CARRY IT OUT:** Depending on the situation, you can try to get out on your own, get out with the help of others, or send for help.

SELF-RESCUE WITH ASSISTANCE

If you are in a group and are injured, you might be able to get out with the assistance of your friends. However, for this to work the injured person must be willing and able to help himself. You also need to consider whether self-rescue would make existing injuries worse. For example, if someone is suffering from an injury such as a fractured vertebra, moving that person could cause additional injury.

If you choose to get out with the help of friends, consider the following when you make your plan:

—Look at the route and choose the easiest way out.

—Realize that the easiest route is not necessarily the shortest, but the one that is best for the injured person.

—Have other people carry the injured person's gear; their job is to get themselves out.

—Have one person stay with the injured person to provide support and monitor their condition.

—Consider whether you can send one person ahead for help to arrange assistance as quickly as possible.

ACCIDENT
MANAGEMENT

"But life had a strong hold on him; in spite of the gale, the volleys of stones, the fearsome cold, he survived the night, swinging backwards and forwards in his rope sling."

—Heinrich Harrer

Left: Accidents are best avoided by paying attention to a number of factors such as physical fitness, proper clothing and adequate gear.

ACCIDENT
MANAGEMENT
(continued)

GETTING OUTSIDE HELP

If an injury is severe, is internal, or involves the head or neck, outside help will be required. Consider the following when making plans to secure assistance.

• **AVAILABILITY OF HELP:** If an accident happens in the summer, for example, when forest fires might be burning, all helicopters can be otherwise engaged. Rescuers may not be able to come immediately due to previous commitments, other ongoing search and rescue, poor weather, or other constraints.

• **HAVE ONE PERSON STAY BEHIND WITH THE INJURED PARTY:** Since it could be a day or two before help arrives, this person should look after the injured person's immediate needs for first aid, warmth, shelter, food, and hydration.

• **SEND TWO PEOPLE FOR HELP:** After the injured have been given first aid, and further help is not required at the accident location, send people for help–two if they are available. The people who go for help should be physically and psychologically capable of getting out by themselves. If you go for help, take your pack in case you need some emergency items yourself.

• **ENSURE PEOPLE GOING FOR HELP HAVE THE APPROPRIATE INFORMATION:** The people who go need to take coins for the telephone or car keys for vehicles. They should be able to provide rescuers with information about:

—Accident location

—Nature of the accident

—Number of people involved

—Extent of the injuries

—What first aid was given

—The distance from the accident site

—The party's strength and experience

—The victim(s) name and address and the telephone numbers of those to be notified in an emergency

• **MARK THE AREA:** Using whatever resources are available such as rocks, tree branches and spare equipmen to mark the location so rescuers can easily see it.

• **GET OUT QUICKLY BUT CAREFULLY:** In the stress of the moment, the people who go for help may get themselves in an accident. Move with careful haste.

• **MARK THE ROUTE ON THE WAY OUT:** Unless the people who go for help are very familiar with the area, or certain that they can find their way back without difficulty, have them mark the route.

• **CONTACT THE APPROPRIATE AUTHORITIES:** In the United States, notify park rangers if the accident has occurred in a national park; otherwise notify the state police. In Canada, notify the Royal Canadian Mounted Police if on provincial land or Parks Canada if in a national park.

• **BE PREPARED TO COME BACK WITH RESCUERS:** The person who reports the accident generally returns to the accident location with the rescuers. The rescuers then evaluate the situation, and decide whether evacuation is to be done by helicopter, snowmobile, or other means.

"I knew that people sometimes died climbing mountains. But at the age of twenty-three, personal mortality—the idea of my own death—was still largely outside my conceptual grasp."

—Jon Krakauer

Two-and Four-Legged Search and Rescue Teams

Jeff Sparhawk and Kiyla

An interview with Jeff Sparhawk, a member of Colorado's Front Range Rescue Dogs.

Why do people in the wilderness need to be rescued?

JS: If everyone had good navigation skills, many of our searches would not have to happen. Wilderness navigation is one of the most important skills to have in the backcountry. People should get a map and compass and learn how to use them before venturing far from their vehicles. And they should not rely upon a cellular phone or a GPS. Batteries go dead, and cellular phone coverage is poor at best. A GPS can spit out some number that represents where you are—but what good does that do if you do not know where you want to be?

Another common occurrence is people who try to hike too far or underestimate their return time.

They end up hiking in the dark, and they may not have the gear to spend the night out. As soon as it gets dark, their family or friends report them as "overdue."

How did you and Kiyla learn to communicate so effectively?

JS: Well, I have been applying the human communication skills I learned in college to the inter-species communication required of any search dog team. I rely on Kiyla's special observational abilities—her nose and ears—and she takes direction from me about where we search.

What requirements did Kiyla have to meet before she could do search and rescue?

JS: In our team—Front Range Rescue Dogs—all dogs must pass a strict obedience test to qualify. They must also pass a trailing test or a series of air scent tests. Trailing dogs follow the scent that the

lost person left on the ground. This can be very difficult depending on how long ago this happened and how many other people crossed the scent trail. Air scent dogs sample the wind and typically search back and forth in a grid pattern. They "look" for the person's scent that is being carried by the wind. When they detect a strong enough scent they follow the scent to its source. Then, they come back and lead the handler to the person. After passing these tests, the dog can go on to specialize in searching avalanches, searching water, or searching for evidence and searching in disasters.

What requirements did you have to meet before you could do search and rescue work?

JS: All of the operational members of Front Range Rescue Dogs must complete a check-off sheet to show they have adequately demonstrated the skills necessary to assist on a search. After this, they must complete a real-time test, which involves working with a dog team in a practice scenario. Before becoming a handler though, a person usually acts as an operational support member, and goes on searches with handlers and helps them with navigation and medical and safety support. Front Range Rescue Dogs usually requires people to do this for a year before allowing them to test their dog and become a handler. We do this to give them some experience on real searches before they try to field a dog at the same time.

ALTITUDE
ILLNESSES

ALTITUDE ILLNESSES

People can experience altitude illnesses when they ascend to elevations of 8,000 feet / 2,400 meters or higher. This occurs mainly because the concentration of oxygen in the blood decreases as elevation increases. As elevation increases, atmospheric pressure decreases. The concentration of oxygen also decreases. At an elevation of 18,000 feet / 5,500 meters, atmospheric and oxygen pressure are half what they are at sea level. The composition of the atmosphere, however, remains the same. Some 20% of the atmosphere is composed of oxygen.

At high elevations, where the pressure of oxygen in the atmosphere is lower, the concentration of oxygen in the blood is also lower. This effects the functioning of the human body. The heart pumps a lower volume of blood at higher altitudes than it does at sea level. The lungs provide less oxygen to the red blood cells. Breathing is more strenuous at high altitudes because more air is moved in and out of the lungs in a reflex compensation mechanism. Getting adequate sleep is more difficult at high altitudes since people breathe less deeply when they are asleep and cannot obtain the oxygen required.

Quickly ascending to higher elevations can result in altitude illnesses such as mild or acute mountain sickness, high altitude pulmonary edema and high altitude cerebral edema. Symptoms of mountain sickness include headache, nausea, weakness, shortness of breath and fatigue. In severe forms of altitude illness, the combination of high altitude and low pressure causes fluid to seep from the capillaries and build up in the lungs (pulmonary edema) and/or brain (cerebral edema). Severe high altitude illness can involve a combination of both pulmonary and cerebral edema.

Because different ranges of elevation have different effects on the body, elevation is generally classified in three levels: high altitude, very high altitude, and extreme altitude. High altitude ranges from 8,000-14,000 feet / 2,400-4,300 meters, while very high altitude ranges from 14,000-18,000 feet / 4,300-5,500 meters. Extreme altitude ranges from 18,000-29,000 feet / 5,500-8,800 meters. Staying at extreme altitude for extended periods of time inevitably results in physical deterioration. Ascending to very high altitude without giving the body time to adjust can result in any form of altitude illness. Ascending to high altitude can cause mild or acute mountain sickness and sometimes results in the more severe forms of altitude illnesses.

Although usually it is only mountaineers who experience very high or extreme altitude, the average hiker or skier in the United States and Canada can experience high altitude—elevations ranging from 8,000-14,000 feet / 2,400-4,300 meters. For example, Colorado has more high peaks than any other state except Alaska. The highest peak in Colorado is Mt. Elbert, reaching a height of 14,433 feet / 4,399 meters. You can experience a rapid elevation gain just by driving from the lowest point in Colorado—3,350 feet / 1,021 meters above sea level on the eastern border of the state—to higher points such as Fall River Pass at an elevation of 11,794 feet / 3,495 meters.

It is difficult to predict who might succumb to altitude illnesses. People who are apparently physically fit and those who are not can suffer from altitude illnesses. It is unpredictable and may occur in people who are acclimatized to altitude. According to *Medicine for Mountaineering,* younger people are more likely to develop high altitude pulmonary edema or acute mountain sickness than those who are older than age 25.

"What is a man on an ice-world up in the sky? At that altitude he is no more than a will straining in a spent machine."

—Gaston Rebuffat

By ascending slowly, these hikers are allowing their bodies to adjust to higher elevations.

ACCLIMATIZING TO HIGH ALTITUDE

The human body can adapt to the decreased concentration of oxygen in the blood caused by high altitude. Those who climb Mt. Everest, for example, can tolerate an elevation of more than 29,000 feet / 8,800 meters for limited periods of time. High altitude climbers can perform effectively at 18,000 feet / 5,500 meters.

The process of allowing the body to adapt to higher elevations is called acclimatization. The key strategy is to ascend slowly and give the body time to adapt. The body adapts to decreased blood oxygen concentration in complex ways. After several days at high altitude, the volume of respiration increases. Relatively more oxygen is delivered to the lungs and absorbed by the blood. The volume of blood pumped by the heart also increases at high altitude. The number of red blood cells increases and the capacity of the red blood cells to deliver oxygen also increases. The muscles also adapt to decreased concentration of oxygen at high altitude.

PREVENTING ALTITUDE ILLNESSES

To help prevent altitude illnesses, give the body time to adjust to the physiological changes brought about by the decreased oxygen concentration in the blood. Factors such as jet lag, lack of sleep, and cold temperatures can worsen the effects of altitude.

ALTITUDE
ILLNESSES
(continued)

"In the mountains it is unhealthy to let your ego drive you."

—*Chic Scott*

A

ALTITUDE
ILLNESSES
(continued)

- **ASCEND GRADUALLY:** Stay several days at an elevation of about 6,000-8,000 feet / 1,800-2,400 meters if you plan to ascend to high altitudes such as 10,000-14,000 feet / 3,000-4,300 meters. Ascend only 500-1,000 feet / 150-300 meters per day and rest every third day if you plan to ascend to altitudes over 14,000 feet / 4,300 meters. Stay several days at an elevation of 12,000-13,000 feet / 3,700-4,000 meters if you plan to ascend to elevations of 15,000-18,000 feet / 4,600-5,500 meters.

- **SLEEP AT LOWER ELEVATIONS:** Sleep at elevations below 8,000 feet / 2,400 meters if possible. Sleeping at higher elevations increases the possibility of succumbing to altitude illnesses such as high altitude pulmonary edema and acute mountain sickness. If you are ascending to very high altitude or ascending several summits, descend to the lowest possible elevation to sleep.

- **EXERCISE LIGHTLY:** Avoid strenuous exercise upon immediate arrival at a higher altitude than what you're normally used to. Perform only light exercise for the first day. Get adequate rest.

- **DRINK LOTS OF WATER:** Dehydration occurs more quickly at higher elevations and thirst is not a good indicator of how much water is needed. At high altitudes, blood becomes thicker, and more water is required to make it thinner. One high altitude climber compares the need to thin the blood to the oil in a vehicle. When oil gets thicker, the vehicle has to work harder to lubricate the engine.

- **EAT ENOUGH FOOD:** Because of the decreased concentration of oxygen in the blood, the body does not fully use the nutrients in food. With increased elevation and increased activity, more fuel is required to meet energy needs. At very high altitudes, 6,000-9,000 calories can be required everyday for basic sustenance. Although foods high in carbohydrates such as pasta and grains offer quick burning fuel, some research suggests fats are an excellent food source at altitude. Consuming foods high in fat enables sufficient calorie intake.

- **AVOID ALCOHOL AND SLEEPING PILLS:** Substances that decrease respiration such as alcohol may worsen the effects of altitude. Amenities such as saunas, which are available at some hostels, chalets and ski resorts, may help induce a restful night's sleep.

- **RESPOND TO SIGNS OF ALTITUDE ILLNESSES:** Early symptoms of mild mountain sickness include headache, light-headedness and confusion. These may subside with sufficient rest and water intake. Descend to lower altitude as soon as possible if these symptoms become worse. Watch your friends for symptoms of altitude illnesses and ensure they descend to lower altitude if required and seek the medical attention needed.

"Here there was no question that oxygen made a difference .... Best of all there was freedom to think about more than the alternate plod-pant-plod, with ten breaths per plod; there was freedom to enjoy the view, and to have thoughts to be alone with."

—Thomas F. Hornbein

ANIMAL BITES
See RABIES.

AVALANCHES
A snow avalanche occurs when a mass of snow is released and slides down a slope. The mass can include other debris such as ice or rocks. Every year, mountain adventurers are injured or killed by these moving bodies of snow; people themselves trigger about 95% of avalanche accidents, many of which could be prevented if those involved had a basic understanding of the precautions to take while traveling in avalanche terrain.

TYPES OF AVALANCHES
There are two main types of avalanches: Wet and dry. Wet avalanches include sluffs and slabs while dry avalanches include sluffs, slabs, and cornice break-offs.

• **CORNICE BREAK OFF:** When a cornice fractures and plummets down the slope below, it can bury people below and may trigger an avalanche.

• **ICE AVALANCHE:** When a glacier moves over a cliff or steep slope, blocks of snow and ice form unstable masses called seracs. When these topple, an ice avalanche occurs. Ice can also fall off mountainsides due to solar warming or other factors. This can trigger avalanches too.

A

ANIMAL BITES

AVALANCHES

High Altitude Illnesses

ACUTE MOUNTAIN SICKNESS

Symptom	Treatment
• Headache	• Drink more fluids to prevent dehydration
• Dizziness	• Take deep breaths unless nausea develops
• Shortness of breath	• Slow down your pace if active, or rest
• Weakness	• Descend to lower elevation if symptoms continue or
• Nausea	become worse
	• Seek medical aid

HIGH ALTITUDE PULMONARY EDEMA

Symptom	Treatment
• Headache	• Immediately descend to lower altitudes if pul-
• Difficulty breathing	monary edema is suspected
• Tightness in the chest	• Monitor the breathing of the victim especially at
• Dizziness	night
• Weakness	• Provide rescue breathing as necessary
• Nausea	• Seek medical aid
• Anxiety	

HIGH ALTITUDE CEREBRAL EDEMA

Symptom	Treatment
• Headache	• Must immediately descend to lower elevations
• Weakness	• Life-threatening; the victim may fall into a coma
• Confusion or psychotic behavior	within a day
• Disorientation	• Provide rescue breathing if necessary
• Unconsciousness	• Seek medical aid

Routefinding is an important aspect of traveling safely in avalanche terrain.

AVALANCHES
(continued)

• **LOOSE SNOW SLIDE:** This type of slide occurs when a small mass of snow, lacking cohesion, releases from a point on the slope. The slide picks up more snow as it continues down the slope and spreads out in the form of a triangle. In these slides, only the top layers of snow are released. These occur mainly on steeper slopes.

• **SLAB AVALANCHE:** When one or more layers of snow fracture from the slope, a slab avalanche occurs. The snow may be either wet or dry. It may also be hard or soft. Slab avalanches vary in size. They may only be a few inches thick or they may be quite deep and encompass a mile or more of terrain. Slab avalanches can occur on moderately angled (skiable) slopes as well as steeper terrain. Nearly all serious avalanches involving people are slab avalanches.

Learning how to identify and avoid avalanche terrain are the first steps in learning how to travel safely in avalanche terrain. Taking a course on avalanche safety from a qualified professional is essential. After that, you need to apply what you have learned to the backcountry. Making appropriate decisions about where or when to travel is a skill that is gained by experience. Search and rescue techniques should be practiced regularly. The information below is provided as a basic introduction to avalanche safety; but it is no substitute for experience and practice.

BEFORE VENTURING INTO AVALANCHE COUNTRY

• **CHECK AVALANCHE BULLETINS:** The United States Forest Service in the United States, and Parks Canada and the Canadian Avalanche Association in Canada provide information to the public about potential avalanche hazards. Their bulletins provide information about the weather, snowpack, and observed avalanche activity. Based on this, the bulletins rate the avalanche hazard using a five-point international scale consisting of designations such as low, moderate, considerable, high and extreme. They also advise backcountry adventurers of recommended actions for traveling in avalanche terrain. Since avalanche danger varies from area to area, bulletins are provided for each major park or mountainous area. Before you go on your trip, obtain a recent avalanche bulletin for the area you plan to visit. It will give you an overall assessment of the terrain and help guide decisions on travel there.

AVALANCHES
(c o n t i n u e d)

• **CHECK THE WEATHER:** Since weather creates most of the necessary conditions for avalanches to occur, it has been called the "architect" of avalanches. Obtain a weather forecast for your proposed trip before you go. The interplay of factors such as temperature, precipitation and wind in creating avalanches is complex. However, here are the basic components.

—**SNOW:** Most avalanches that occur naturally happen during or shortly after a storm. This is because the snowpack has not had enough time to accommodate the weight of the newly fallen snow. When the snowpack is rapidly loaded with large amounts of new snow, the hazard increases. In time, the buried weak layers will adjust to their load and become more stable.

—**RAIN:** Unlike snow, rain does not strengthen the snowpack. It washes away the bonding of the layers in the snowpack. Over time, the snowpack freezes and strengthens. However, when another snowfall occurs, the crust becomes a sliding surface for the new and subsequent layers of snowfall.

—**WIND:** Wind picks up snow on windward slopes and then deposits it on leeward ones. In this process, wind helps create cornices and pillows of snow on lee slopes. The direction of the prevailing winds causes certain slopes to regularly become wind-loaded. Wind can deposit snow 10 times more rapidly than snow falling from the sky. Wind is usually the most important weather factor. Thin weak layers and the development of depth hoar characterize wind-loaded slopes. Lee slopes are characterized by thick, poorly bonded layers and favor the development of cornices.

—**SUDDEN WARM TEMPERATURES:** The temperature of the snowpack is determined in part by the temperature of the air, the radiant energy of the sun, and the radiant energy that the snow reflects back into the atmosphere. Changes in temperature affect the mechanical properties of the layers and thus the stability of the snowpack. This is especially apparent when a sudden warming trend occurs after an extended period of cold weather.

—**SOLAR RADIATION:** The radiant energy of the sun can weaken the snowpack. In the spring, rising temperatures can melt the snow surface causing water to percolate through the snowpack. The bonds between the grains of snow weaken and loose snow or slab avalanches may occur.

"If you have to cross the slope one at a time, you should not be there."

—Bruce Tremper

• **CHECK EQUIPMENT:** Review all equipment before setting off into potential avalanche country.

—**TRANSCEIVERS:** If you plan to travel in avalanche terrain, take transceivers, shovels and probes and know how to use them. Transceivers

AVALANCHES
(continued)

continually emit a signal. When someone is buried, the survivors or rescuers turn their transceivers to "Receive." The signal of the buried person gets louder the closer you get. The 457kHZ frequency is the standard in North America. Some transceivers also offer other features such as an external speaker with a distinct signal, a flashing visual indicator to assist in pinpointing when searching, and battery strength indicators. When planning a backcountry trip, make sure everyone in the group has compatible transceivers.

—**SHOVELS:** A shovel is an essential piece of equipment to clear avalanche debris. Avalanche shovels have a removable handle so they are easier to pack. Shovels made from aluminum are considered the best. Remember too, you can also use a shovel to make a snow shelter in an emergency.

—**PROBES:** A probe is equally necessary when traveling in avalanche terrain. It consists of a number of aluminum tubes that can be quickly assembled to form one long unit. This is used to probe deep below the surface of the snow to detect where someone might be buried. Two-part ski poles are also available that can be assembled to make an avalanche probe. Probe poles are convenient but much shorter than a conventional probe and they are more difficult to assemble—a significant drawback when every minute counts.

• **DISCUSS THE TRIP WITH YOUR GROUP:** Research the route to discover whether there are any known dangers such as cornices and avalanche terrain. After gathering this information, discuss the proposed route with your backcountry partners and get consensus on the overall plan. The group needs to evaluate the danger of the avalanche terrain they plan on crossing that day by assessing factors such as steepness, anchors, consequences and aspect. Have an alternative trip in mind in case conditions change making your first choice unadvisable.

• **ON YOUR TRIP, EVALUATE THE AVALANCHE TERRAIN:** The work done in planning your trip gives you a good indication of what the conditions might be like on your route. However, this is just an overall assessment of a particular region. Once you get out there, you may find conditions change from valley to valley. This is because microclimates occur in different locales. As a result, you need to assess the conditions continually as you travel. The first thing to do is to evaluate any slopes:

Indications of Avalanche Instability

When traveling in avalanche terrain observe conditions around you. All of the signs listed below indicate that the snowpack is not stable and may slide. Backcountry skiers notice some of these signs more than snowmobilers since their proximity to the snow enables them to get in touch with the way it looks, sounds, and feels.

• **Recent avalanches on similar slopes:** If slopes similar to the one you plan to ski have slid, this is an indication your slope can slide too.

• **Hollow sounds:** A weak layer, lying under a stronger layer, can cause you to hear a drum-like sound. A hollow sound indicates the presence of an unstable slab.

• **"Whumphing" sounds:** When weak layers within the snowpack collapse, a sudden "whumphing" sound may occur. This is a sign of extreme instability.

• **Shooting cracks:** If cracks begin to branch out in the snow around you, the snowpack is unstable.

—**RECENT AVALANCHE ACTIVITY:** This is by far the most important stability indicator. Check slopes of similar steepness and angle to see if there is evidence of recent avalanche activity. If similar slopes have slid, the slope you intend to ski, board or ride will likely slide too.

—**PAST AVALANCHE ACTIVITY:** If a slope has slid before, it can slide again. A treeless slope, sandwiched between forested areas, is an indication of past avalanche activity. So is a slope having shorter trees in the center and taller trees on the edges. Trees with broken branches on the uphill side also indicate past slide activity.

—**ANGLE OF THE SLOPE:** Consider whether the slope is steep enough to slide. Slab avalanches generally occur in slopes ranging from 25-60 degrees. Slopes of a lesser angle are not usually steep enough to slide while slopes over 60 degrees are so steep that snow does not adhere. Most slab avalanches occur in slopes between 30-45 degrees. This is about the same angle that most people like to ski.

—**SHAPE OF THE SLOPE**: Consider whether the slope is convex, concave or smooth. Convex slopes are most likely to break just below the hump because this is where the stress of the snowpack is greatest. Conversely, a concave slope may be more stable at the base than a convex one because the weight of the snow compresses the snowpack. However, avalanches can still occur on concave slopes. A smooth slope can avalanche at any point if conditions are favorable. A slope can also break just below a terrain feature such as a cliff.

—**ANCHORS:** Rocks, trees and other features, situated closely together and visible above the snow, help secure the snow to the slope. These slopes are less likely to slide than ones with no anchors. However, when buried, terrain features no longer anchor the snow to the slope. The snow may even begin to slide near these features because they place stress upon the snowpack.

—**DIRECTION OF THE SLOPE:** Wind deposits snow on leeward slopes and increase the stress on the snowpack. As a result, these slopes can slide more easily than windward slopes. There is usually less snow on windward slopes than leeward ones. Where wind is not a factor, either windward or leeward slopes may slide. During the winter, the north-facing slopes are more dangerous and during the wet spring slide times, south facing slopes are more dangerous.

—**CHECK THE STABILITY OF THE SNOWPACK:** Most of the serious avalanches involving people are slab avalanches. Potential for a slab avalanche exists when a weak layer forms under a strong layer, or the strong layer is not well bonded to the weak layer. If the layer is weak, the individual grains of snow within it are not well bonded while the opposite occurs in a strong layer. If these conditions exist on a slope that is steep enough to slide and the snowpack is not stable, a slab avalanche may occur. Perform a snow stability test such as a shovel shear test, a compression test, or a Rutschblock. If you are not familiar with these tests, perform a ski pole test. This test can be performed easily and quickly if the snowpack is too deep. You can use it throughout your trip to test the snow continually and see if it is changing.

AVALANCHES
(continued)

"The mountaineer sets off promising himself to regulate his pace carefully to his breathing: However he soon lacks air, for the air is so poor that it no longer feeds the machine."

— Gaston Rebuffat

AVALANCHES
(continued)

—**SKI POLE TEST:** To do this test, hold the basket end of your ski pole at a 90 degree angle to the surface of the snow. (If the snow is very hard, use the other end of the pole.) As you push it beneath the surface, take note of the different layers. Some can be weaker than others. Make the hole larger by moving your pole in a circle. When the hole is sufficiently large, feel the different layers using your fingers. Doing this test helps you discover whether weak layers are present under stronger layers. This helps you evaluate the stability of the snowpack.

•**DECIDE WHETHER TO TRAVEL ON THE SLOPE:** After looking at the angle and stability of the slope, consider factors such as weather and group comfort. Put all of this information together to make a decision about the slope.

TRAVELING IN AVALANCHE TERRAIN

1. Avalanches can release from a point high above you. Travel well back from steep chutes and other potential release points instead of directly under them.

2. A slope lacking trees or having small stunted trees shows evidence of past avalanches. Choose a route through larger trees, dense forest, or along the valley bottom well back from potential avalanche slopes.

3. Avalanches can occur in bowls with deposits of wind-loaded snow or in gullies that funnel snow. Avoid these areas when avalanche hazard exists or when in doubt. Travel on ridges because they provide a safer route above bowls and gullies. Avoid routes that cut into bowls from the sides.

4. Cornices can break and trigger an avalanche. On ridges, travel well back from the cornice. In valleys, avoid traveling directly under the probable path of a falling cornice.

5. Slopes that curve inward can have a weak point below the top. Cross convex slopes well below the point of weakness.

6. Cliffs, boulders, and other outcrops can create a weak point in the snow pack. Travel well back from such terrain features instead of directly under or beside them.

7. A skier traveling directly below can undercut slopes that curve inwards. Cross concave slopes well back from potential release points.

—WEATHER: After you have assessed the relative danger of the avalanche terrain, check your current conditions. Has the weather changed since you started your trip? If it is windy and starting to snow the stress on the snowpack will increase.

—COMFORT LEVEL: Also check the comfort level of your group. Everyone has a personal risk threshold. Some may not want to cross or ski a certain slope. Their judgement must be honored. In the excitement of wanting to ski a wonderful powder slope, some people can seem to experience a type of amnesia and forget warning signals. The one person expressing discomfort with the slope may be the only sane person in the group. Be aware of the "herding instinct"—the idea that you are somehow safe simply because you are with other people.

—EXISTING TRACKS: If you see tracks from a skier, boarder or snowmobiler, do not assume the slope is stable because others have crossed it. Although the snowpack could have been relatively stable when they crossed it, conditions change. The stress of one more skier or boarder may be enough to cause the snow to fracture.

—RUN-OUT: Take a good look at the surrounding terrain. If you were caught in an avalanche, where might you end up?

—SAFER ROUTES: If the stability of the slope is suspect, choose a route that offers the least amount of risk. If possible, keep to the floor of the valley, well away from potential slide paths. Ascend a ridge and avoid dangerous terrain such as slopes occurring under a cornice, steep lee bowls or gullies. Instead of traveling on an open slope, ski or board in forested areas. Choose to ride a low angle slope rather than a steep one.

• CROSSING AVALANCHE SLOPES: Avalanche experts advise certain precautions to decrease risk while crossing any potential avalanche slope—whether you think it is stable or not. "If you feel you need to take these precautions before you cross a slope, you should not be there in the first place," cautions Bruce Tremper, Utah avalanche specialist.

—UNBUCKLE YOUR EQUIPMENT: If an avalanche occurs, you will want to discard equipment such as ski poles and skis as quickly as possible because they will weigh you down or cause injuries. To facilitate this, unfasten the straps on your ski poles and any "runaway" straps on skis before you cross the slope. If you are carrying a heavy pack, unfasten the hip belt. If you have a light pack, keep it fastened as it may help to prevent back injuries.

—ZIP UP: If you are wearing a jacket, zip it up snugly around your neck. Tuck mittens inside your sleeves, and put your hat on. If you are caught in a slide, doing this prevents snow from getting inside your clothes, weighing you down and making you cold and wet.

—DECIDE UPON A PLAN: Before crossing, assess the route and decide upon an escape route if the slope slides. Decide who is going to cross the slope first and where everyone will wait once they have crossed.

AVALANCHES
(continued)

—CROSS ONE AT A TIME: Do not have more than one person on the slope at a time. The combined weight of more than one person can load the slope and cause it to slide. In addition, if it does slide, and everyone is caught in it, no one will be available to rescue the victims. Instead, cross a hazardous slope one at a time, and do it quickly. The less time you spend in a hazardous place, the better. Do not stop in a potential slide path.

After the snow slides, it hardens quickly into cement-like clumps called avalanche debris.

—WATCH THE PERSON WHO IS CROSSING: Since avalanches happen quickly, you can quickly lose sight of a person who is caught in an avalanche if you are not watching carefully. Observe the person until they are safely across the slope. If an avalanche occurs, it is crucial to know the "last seen" point of the victim.

—WAIT IN A SAFE PLACE: After you have crossed the suspect slope, make sure you are well away from the potential slide path. If you cross an open slope into some trees, get well back into the trees. Although the presence of dense forest usually indicates safety, avalanches can also sweep through thickly treed slopes.

AVALANCHE SURVIVAL

If you are caught in an avalanche, you can do certain things to increase your chances of survival. Essentially, you are attempting to avoid burial and stay on top or close to the surface.

"If you are caught in a light avalanche and you are wearing a light pack, keep it on. It can protect your back. If you have a heavy pack, get rid of it."

— Lloyd Gallagher

• **SHOUT:** Call out to your group so they will know you need help. By watching you, they can get a better idea of the direction the slide takes you and make an informed decision about where you may be buried. This will also help them locate your "last point seen."

• **DISCARD EQUIPMENT:** If you can, get rid of your skis, poles or snowboard. Heavy equipment weighs you down. Your chances of staying on top are better if you are lighter. Also, the likelihood of injuring yourself is higher if you are wearing equipment such as skis since they will get caught in the avalanche and thrash you around.

• **STAY ON TOP:** Using swimming motions, try to stay on top of the avalanche. If you are near the surface, you might be able to keep your head or hands above the surface of the snow. Try to "swim" to the side of the avalanche. The snow can be less deep on the perimeter.

These skiers are keeping well away from the potential avalanche hazard on the treeless slopes.

This narrow canyon is a "terrain trap;" snow-laden slopes can slide and trap the skier in the bottom of the canyon.

• **POKE A HAND OUT:** As the avalanche stops, push your way towards the surface and thrust a hand out. Getting a hand above the snow will help rescuers find you quickly.

• **CREATE AN AIR SPACE:** Using your other hand, make breathing spaces in front of your face.

AVALANCHES
(continued)

• **AVOID STRUGGLING:** If you can see light coming through the snow, you might be able to poke your head or arms to the surface. Otherwise, it is unlikely that you will be able to get out, since snow is very heavy. Try to relax. This helps conserve energy and save oxygen.

SEARCHING FOR AVALANCHE VICTIMS

You are your friend's best hope of survival. About half of the people completely buried by an avalanche do not survive for more than 20 minutes. If you are in the backcountry and you skied out for help, your friend would perish by the time help arrived—you are the help. Thus it is important to know the basics of avalanche search and rescue. Some people venture into the wilderness without transceivers. If you do not have them, search for your friend using probes. However, the chance of finding someone buried by using only probes is very low.

• **TAKE AN AVALANCHE COURSE AND PRACTICE A SEARCH:** Although it can look relatively straightforward, things have a tendency to get complicated very quickly when an accident occurs. The basic steps are outlined below.

• **ENSURE YOUR OWN SAFETY:** If one avalanche has occurred, another one could happen at any time. Will the slope slide again? Depending on the degree of hazard, you might consider not risking your own life to save another.

• **PLAN YOUR STRATEGY:** Assess your situation and come up with a basic plan. It does not have to be complicated. Making a plan helps you avoid having people all over the slope, possibly creating further problems. Plan your escape route ahead of time.

People often mistakenly believe their level of safety increases if they are in a group. The opposite can be true in avalanche terrain.

AVALANCHES
(continued)

• **POST A LOOKOUT:** If you are in a large group, you could have someone watch the slope for further slide activity.

• **MARK THE "LAST SEEN" POINT:** Where did you last see the victim(s) before they got caught? Knowing this point helps you establish the parameters of the search area. Some people also wear avalanche cords. This 100-foot / 30-meter long cord trails behind the skier. Theoretically, if an avalanche occurs, the cord floats above the snow and allows rescuers to quickly pinpoint the location of the victim. Avalanche cords have performed effectively for this purpose but they are not effective 100% of the time. Critics of avalanche cords point out that the entire cord could be dragged under the snow. Once buried, it is of little use in locating the victim. However, some people carry avalanche cords as a back-up device. If their transceiver fails, they at least have the reassurance of knowing they are trailing a cord.

• **SEARCHING WITH TRANSCEIVERS:** Consider the last seen point of the victim and his/her likely path of travel. Look for clues on the surface such as a glove or hat while you are searching. Do not clutter the slope with the rescuers' possessions.

• **SWITCH TO "RECEIVE:"** Avalanche transceivers have two settings: "Transmit," which sends a signal, and "Receive," which accepts a signal. Since the victim's transceiver is on transmit, you need to switch to "Receive" to pick up the signal.

• **SPREAD OUT:** If people in your group have transceivers with speakers rather than earphones, picking up a signal can be confusing. Spread out at intervals of 100 feet / 30 meters to avoid this problem and to cover the territory.

• **LISTEN FOR A SIGNAL:** If you get a signal, progressively narrow the search territory by turning down the volume on your transceiver. If your party is large enough, one or two people can continue searching if there are other victims. You need to practice regularly. People who do not practice will probably not be able to find someone in time to save their life.

• **PROBE FOR THE VICTIM:** Once you have defined a small area, probe for the victim. Once you have located the victim, dig out the face and chest first. Leave the probe in place to ensure the burial point is identified. To avoid injuring the victim, see the material on "Providing First Aid."

• **TURN OFF THE VICTIM'S TRANSCEIVER:** If there are other people buried, switch the victim's transceiver from transmit to receive. This reduces confusion.

• **SEARCHING WITH A PROBE LINE:** If you do not have transceivers, probe for the victim(s) using avalanche probes, ski poles, skis, or other available equipment. First, probe the "last seen" point of the victim.

AVALANCHES
(continued)

Recognizing the "Human Factor"

Dr. Bruce Jamieson

In learning how to travel safely in avalanche terrain, backcountry adventurers study factors such as the angle of the slope, the weather, and the stability of the snowpack. Yet many of them forget one significant aspect: the role people play in triggering avalanches or the so-called "human factor."

Dr. Bruce Jamieson, co-author of *Avalanche Accidents in Canada: 1984 to 1996,* says, "The human factor is the most overlooked factor in avalanche education." With 20 years of experience in avalanche research and a past president of the Canadian Avalanche Association, he is in a good position to assess the importance of this factor.

"Some avalanche accidents have occurred because the people involved did not recognize the danger," explains Jamieson. "However, in other cases, they did recognize it but decide to keep going anyway."

What are some of the common reasons why people continue despite the known hazard? One major issue is the "herding instinct." People tend to think they are safe when they are in a group. But the opposite is true when traveling in avalanche terrain because the danger increases with the size of the group.

The avalanche specialist says personality dynamics also play a role. "You may have some keener way out in front breaking trail when the people with the smarts are in the back of the group." By driving ahead without fully assessing the surroundings, the keeners may lead the others into dangerous terrain. In addition, those who are forceful or overly confident may not listen to those with a quiet manner even though they have the most experience.

Furthermore, people who work in the city all week at stressful jobs are often on a tight timetable. They want to achieve their objective—a pass, a summit or a long trip—and be back in time for work on Monday morning. Pushed by this "city time" mentality, people may ski or ride out in dangerous conditions instead of respecting "mountain time" and waiting for circumstances to improve.

How can mountain adventurers be made more aware of the important role the human factor plays in avalanche accidents? One way, says Jamieson, is for backcountry travelers to deal with this issue both before and during the trip.

Jamieson also notes that the general tendency of backcountry travelers is to travel in small groups of peers. In this situation, he advises all of the group members to get together during the trip to discuss the major route finding and stability questions. In this way, all assume part of the responsibility. Each member of the group should continue to assume responsibility when out in the backcountry.

Generally speaking, however, the tendency of people to push on even though they recognize the danger is a matter of their emotions overruling their judgement. Excited by the prospect of a new route or a summit, they seem to forget their training. It may also be a matter of pride or simply pure excitement. "Skiing or boarding in powder snow is euphoric," explains Jamieson. "We need to deliberately switch to a decision-making mode."

Assessing Stability:

Assessing slope stability is a critical factor while traveling in avalache terrain.

small mountain range. In my work on individual slopes, I found there was an incredible amount of variability in any given snowslope. A number of factors such as what exists beneath the snowpack, the trees on the slope, and the patterns of radiation and wind are causes of this.

What about a larger area such as a mountain range? Is the stability much the same throughout?

KB: Well, in my larger scale research in the Bridger Range of Montana, I was basically trying to analyze the patterns of stability over a small mountain range on one given day. So I had 12 different sampling teams and we went out and dug over 70 different snow pits on each of two different sampling days. On the days that I sampled, there was a pattern of more unstable conditions in higher elevations and on more northerly facing aspects.

Do the overall patterns for a mountain range stay much the same for a season? Or do they vary?

KB: Those patterns are always changing all the time. And that is why my research just basically gave us a couple of snapshots of the system. But the dynamics of the system are still unexplored. We need to do further research about how fast some of these patterns change, and how they change every day or over the course of the season. We can make some assumptions about how that happens, but no one has actually quantified it yet.

A conversation with Karl Birkeland, an avalanche specialist at the Gallatin National Forest Avalanche Center, Montana, who has done extensive research on snowpack stability.

What does your research indicate about the stability of a slope? Is it much the same throughout?

KB: In my research, I looked at both the variability of snowpack properties over an individual slope and the variability over a

Will the Slope Slide?

What implications does your research on snowpack stability have for backcountry travelers? What about snowpits? Does digging a good pit indicate the slope is stable?

KB: Well, I have heard, "You can use a snowpit to tell you the snow is unstable but you should not use it to tell you the snow is stable." In other words, if you dig a snowpit and the snow looks unstable, that is a good indication there are unstable locations on the slope and you might trigger an avalanche. However, if you dig a snowpit and the snow is relatively stable, that does not necessarily mean there is not some unstable area on that slope where you could trigger an avalanche.

Why is a snowpit not a fail-proof method of determining stability? Is the location a factor?

KB: Where you dig the pit is very important. I have been out on days when you could trigger an avalanche just about anywhere, and I have dug a snowpit in the wrong place and the snow has looked pretty darn good.

Does it matter whether you dig it on the side of the slope or on the bottom?

KB: The best place to dig a snowpit is in an area representative of the middle of the slope that could fracture. You want to get a clear picture of the relationship between the various layers in the snowpack where you might trigger an avalanche and that would

tend to be mid-slope. Of course, you can't just go right to the middle of the slope because you could trigger an avalanche. So, you try to find a place where the conditions are similar to the area where you think a slide could be triggered, but is still safe.

What about digging a snowpit on the top of the slope?

KB: Bruce Jamieson (a Canadian avalanche specialist) has done some research that shows you might not want to dig your snowpit at the very top of a slope especially if it has been exposed to wind. His work has shown that people who have dug slopes at the very top have sometimes overestimated the stability of the slopes. If I am in an open slope with trees on both sides, I will sometimes go into the trees and dig somewhere towards the middle of the slope, but it all depends on the particular slope. A lot of it is based on experience.

What about the number of pits? Is one enough? Or is three required?

KB: I do not think there is anyone who has been around avalanches for a long time who would tell you that, if you dug one snowpit and it looks stable, that you would just say, okay, the slope looks stable. You cannot really say that assessing the stability of a particular slope takes three snowpits or something like that because it depends on the slope and where you dig those three snowpits. If you dig them all in inappropriate locations, you still

will not have an indication of how stable the slope is. On the other hand, you could go to a slope and dig one snowpit and that one snowpit might be in a perfect location and it might give you a very good idea of what the stability is. It is difficult to describe how to assess the stability of the snowpack in a short interview. So if you want to learn, it is a good idea to take some avalanche safety classes and get some practice out in the field.

Are there other ways to assess stability other than digging snowpits?

KB: There are a number of obvious signs that warn you the snowpack is not stable. Observing recent avalanche activity, hearing the snowpack collapse (that "whumphing" sound under your skis) and seeing cracks shooting out from your skis or your snowmobile—those are the big three that you see again and again that people ignore and later end up being caught in avalanches. Other important pieces of information are the different layers in your snowpack. If you have been following the snowpack for the whole season, if you know the history of the avalanche activity in your area, if you know what the recent weather has been, and if you know how much stress there is on different layers in the snowpack, you will have a much better idea of the potential avalanche problems you might face in a particular area or on a particular slope.

AVALANCHES
(continued)

—**LOOK FOR CLUES ON THE SURFACE OF THE SNOW:** If you can locate a hat, ski pole, ski, or other item, it can indicate the victim's location. People either discard their equipment when caught in an avalanche to make themselves lighter, or naturally lose equipment with the force of the snow. Thus something belonging to the victim(s) can be found on or near the surface of the snow

—**PROBE NEAR CLUES:** If you find a clue, probe in that area. Use a probe, inverted ski pole, or stick. You might be fortunate and the victim could be nearby. Mark any clues as well as any areas probed.

Recent avalanche activity marks potentially dangerous areas to avoid.

—**PROBE LIKELY AREAS:** Assess the terrain and locate features where the victim may have come to a stop. These include the area below the "last seen" point, and natural features such as large rocks and trees. Look at the slope. Where would the individual come to a stop? At the toe of the avalanche? Along the sides?

—**SET UP A PROBE LINE:** If you have not found the victim through random probing, organize your party in a line. Have three people stand in a line about an arm's length apart. Probe left, then center, and then right, and then move forward one step. If your party is large enough, have someone dig any areas where probers have contacted something. If you are unsuccessful with the first probe line, continue trying.

PROVIDING FIRST AID
Begin by looking after the basic ABCs: Airway, Breathing and Circulation.

"The human factor is the most overlooked factor in avalanche education."

— Bruce Jamieson

• **CLEAR THE MOUTH, NOSE, AND AIRWAY:** If caught in an avalanche and unconscious, the victim's mouth and nose can be clogged with snow. Clear snow away to facilitate breathing since suffocation will be the most likely cause of death during an avalanche. Provide rescue breathing or cardiopulmonary resuscitation if you have the training to do so.

• **BE AWARE OF POSSIBLE INJURY TO THE SPINE:** The victim may have been thrashed around in the avalanche and damaging the spine. When moving the victim, immobilize the back and neck to avoid further spinal injuries. Immobilize the neck of the casualty by using boots to make a U-shaped pillow to fit the head and neck.

• **PROVIDE FIRST AID TO INJURIES:** Check for injuries. If the victim is wearing several layers of clothing, bleeding might not be apparent. However, if bleeding has occurred, stop it by applying direct pressure to the area.

• **TREAT FOR HYPOTHERMIA:** The victim could become hypothermic as a result of direct contact with the snow. Insulate the body from the cold and begin to re-warm; see Hypothermia.

• **START EVACUATION PROCEDURES:** The victim needs immediate medical help. Depending on your location and the number of people in your party, you can choose to send for help or evacuate the victim to a warm and safe place. If you have camping equipment and are a long way from shelter, set up a tent or build a snow shelter. Get the victim(s) into sleeping bags and provide them with hot liquids.

AVALANCHES
(continued)

Avalanche Hazard Scale

The scale below, used by the American Association of Avalanche Professionals, rates the potential for avalanches. However, since it only provides a general guideline, always use your own common sense, knowledge, and judgment in making decisions about travel in avalanche terrain. Hazard varies from place to place depending on factors such as the amount of snowfall and the aspect of the slope. The U.S. scale is based on the international scale that was agreed upon by the International Commission of Alpine Rescue. All countries in the world use this scale (with a few minor exceptions).

Danger Level (and Color)	Avalanche Probability and Avalanche Trigger	Degree and Distribution of Avalanche Danger	Recommended Action in the Backcountry
LOW (green)	Natural avalanches very unlikely. Human-triggered avalanches unlikely.	Generally stable snow. Isolated areas of instability.	Travel is generally safe. Normal caution is advised.
MODERATE (yellow)	Natural avalanches unlikely. Human-triggered avalanches possible.	Unstable slabs possible on steep terrain.	Use caution in steeper terrain on certain aspects.
CONSIDERABLE (orange)	Natural avalanches possible. Human-triggered avalanches probable.	Unstable slabs probable on steep terrain.	Be increasingly cautious in steeper terrain.
HIGH (red)	Natural and human-triggered avalanches likely.	Unstable slabs likely on a variety of aspects and slope angles.	Travel not recommended. Safest on windward ridges of lower angle slopes without steeper terrain above.
EXTREME (black)	Widespread natural or human triggered avalanches certain.	Extremely unstable slabs certain on most aspects and slope angles. Large, destructive avalanches possible.	Travel in avalanche terrain should be avoided and confined to low angle terrain well away avalanche path run-outs.

FEAR: Friend or Foe?

Alan Hobson

An interview with Alan Hobson, a writer, an adventurer and the tenth Canadian to stand on the summit of Mount Everest.

Can fear be your friend in the mountains?

AH: Fear can be one of your greatest assets in the mountains. Fear is your intuition talking to you. I can recall instances, where for reasons I could not explain, I would feel uncomfortable walking across a certain snowslope. I would listen to my intuition and back off—only to find out later the slope had avalanched.

When is fear not your friend?

AH: Fear is a bad thing when it is not rational, and you make irrational decisions because you act out of fear. I believe fear is the number one thing that stops us from achieving our goals—whether in the mountains or in daily life. In the mountains, it is the fear of the unknown, and the fear of making mistakes and suffering disastrous consequences as a result. But I have also discovered that on the other side of fear is freedom.

Can you recall a time when fear was overtaking you?

AH: I remember crossing the Khumbu Icefall on our ascent of Mount Everest in 1997. The icefall is full of huge crevasses, and some of them are 150 feet deep. Ladders are used to cross the crevasses. The ladders are in eight-foot long segments, and they are lashed together with climbing ropes. Once you start to cross, the ladders begin to bow, and they move up, and they move down. Looking down, all you can see is the crevasse descending into darkness.

How did you deal with your fear at that time?

AH. I had a choice at that time to focus on the rungs of the ladder or the dark hole gaping beneath me. I learned quickly that if I looked into that black hole, I would probably end up there. It was a matter of the irrational being managed by the rational, and I have learned that climbing Everest is about 75 % mental work and only about 25% physical work. The ability to make a choice is something that is always 100% within our own control.

What other tools do you use to manage your fear?

AH: Another way to manage fear is to anticipate it and then handle it with knowledge. Assess the challenge that lies before you. Ask yourself if you have the physical and psychological strength required. Ask yourself if you have the equipment you need. Know you have the things you need before setting out, and then you can attack it with knowledge.

Is turning back ever an option?

AH: The decision to turn back is sometimes the best decision, and the one that should be taken. The idea of having mental toughness—of pushing on regardless of the cost—is not a philosophy that I adhere to. In the West, we love to think we can conquer Nature. We think we can conquer mountains, but that can never be done. We can no more conquer Nature than we can conquer a tornado.

Most bears act defensively when they encounter people: they act out of fear.

B E A R S

BEARS

Ursidae, the bear family, includes grizzly bears (*Ursus arctos*), North American black bears (*Ursus americanus*), and polar bears (*Ursus maritimus*) in North America. Since polar bears live primarily in marine habitats along the Arctic Coast, the two species people will most likely encounter in the mountains of North America are the grizzly bear and the black bear.

Being able to identify the different species of bears is useful: Although all bears are dangerous, grizzly bears are more aggressive than black bears. Scientists believe that as black bears evolved, they learned to climb trees to escape from danger. Grizzly bears, on the other hand, adapted to life on the open plains. Since climbing a tree was not an option, they learned to stand their ground and fight.

GRIZZLY BEARS

Although grizzly bears once occupied the western half of North America, their range has been greatly reduced through resource development and human encroachment. Scientists estimate that up to 50,000 grizzlies lived in the contiguous United States some 3,000 years ago. Today, less than 1,000 are estimated to exist in the contiguous United States, occupying about 1% of their former range.

Pockets of grizzly habitat exist in remote, mountainous regions in the northern Rocky Mountains and in the Pacific Northwest in the United States. Grizzly habitat is more continuous in British Columbia, Yukon and Alaska. Some experts estimate that 40,000 grizzlies may survive in Alaska and about 20,000 live in the Yukon and the province of British Columbia.

Unlike the black bear, whose body is round and short, grizzlies have massive shoulder muscles. This gives them a pronounced shoulder hump. They may be brown, black, or blonde in color. Their fur changes in color depending on their age and the season. A grizzly whose fur is silver at the ends is known as a "silvertip." Grizzlies have an upturned muzzle, which gives them a dished or concave facial appearance. Grizzlies have long, tapered claws about 2-4 inches long / 5-10 cm, approximately the length of an average person's fingers.

Black bears, like all bears, are unpredictable.

B E A R S
(continued)

BLACK BEARS

The black bear has a higher population than the grizzly because it has adapted to a wider variety of habitats including foothills, forests and mountainous regions. Although its territory has also been greatly reduced, black bears are found throughout much of North America.

People generally see black bears more often than grizzlies because they adapt more readily to areas occupied by humans. Color and size are not the best indicators of species. Black bears may have black, brown, white, or cinnamon-colored fur. The nose is tapered with long nostrils and the facial profile is straighter than that of a grizzly. Black bears have shorter claws than the grizzly, about 1-1.5 inches / 2.5-4 cm long.

In North America, there are only about six fatalities from bear attacks each year. Although there are hundreds of encounters between people and bears every year, the number of fatalities is quite small. Researchers believe a person's chances of being killed by a bear is about a million to one. However, this does not mean people should be complacent about bears. They are wild, powerful, unpredictable creatures capable of inflicting massive, life-threatening injuries. One blow from a black bear, for example, can kill a deer. A bear attack is dangerous both for the person and the bear: People can get frightened, mauled, or killed, and the bear can get removed, relocated, or destroyed.

Bears are unpredictable and have their own personalities. One bear might be tolerant of people while another may charge with little provocation. Since it is impossible for people to tell whether an encounter with a bear will result in a bluff, attack, mauling, or retreat, the best way to handle a close encounter is to not have one at all.

While bears in the backcountry will usually avoid people, bears that associate food with people lose their fear of humans. Bears that find garbage in a campground will continually return to that campground and may become a nuisance.

Are Bear Attacks on the Rise?

Dr. Stephen Herrero

An interview with Dr. Stephen Herrero, a well known North American expert on bears and author of *Bear Attacks: Their Causes and Avoidance.*

Are bear attacks increasing?

SH: Bear attacks are increasing in areas like British Columbia, Canada, and certainly recent summers have witnessed bear attacks in the province of Alberta. But the reason for the increase in the number of attacks is not 100% clear.

What might be contributing to the increase in bear attacks?

SH: The thing we know the best is that there is a strong correlation between the number of peo-

ple and the number of bears interacting and injuries. I suspect the reason for the increase in injuries especially in British Columbia is due to more people out there logging, mining, hunting, and recreating in various ways.

There has been some discussion about hunting as a means to manage bear attacks. Do you think this would be effective?

SH: Some people have suggested the increase in bear injuries is due to changes in hunting policies and that we are not hunting bears heavily enough or not killing enough bears. I do not see evidence for that. One of the reasons is that three quarters of the grizzly bear inflicted injuries con-

tinue to be by females with young and that is a group we do not hunt. In fact, hunting tries to select strongly for males rather than females. If there were an increase in injuries due to more males or from males then perhaps it might be addressed by changes in hunting.

Could a change in the bears' behavior or our management of them be contributing to the increase in attacks?

SH: Basically, there is no evidence I can find that bears are changing their behavior. This is an issue that I think is important for people to understand. And our food and garbage management continues to get better and better and that decreases the chances of having bears hanging around areas where people are.

I spent some time in Yosemite National Park and met a fellow who had left a peanut butter sandwich in his van. A bear subsequently broke it into whereas our vehicle was left untouched.

SH: The old truth that 'attractant management is the fundamental of bear management' is as true today as ever. If you cannot manage the attractants then you are going to have bear problems just like the person who left the peanut butter sandwich in the car. Generally speaking, the Rocky Mountain national parks in Canada, since 1980, have done an excellent job of managing the attractants.

BEARS
(continued)

HABITAT AND MOVEMENTS

Knowing what bears eat can help people avoid meeting a bear. If people know where they feed, they can either be extra cautious in those areas or avoid them. Although bears are omnivorous, their main diet is vegetable (black bears: 90%; grizzly bears: 80%).

Throughout the day, temperature and availability of food influence bears' movements. Black bears feed in the early morning and evening, and rest during the heat of the day, seeking shade in the dense underbrush. If people bushwhack through thick bushes during the day, they might stumble upon a resting bear. Grizzlies are more active in daylight than black bears. However, they seek relief from mid-day temperatures by resting in "day beds" located in cooler forested areas.

Bears' movements also change depending on the season. In the spring, for example, inland bears concentrate on grasses, succulent shoots, and animals killed over the winter. People might see them on slopes with a southern exposure that are covered with fresh lush vegetation. Use extreme caution when crossing avalanche slopes.

In the summer, when food is more abundant, bears feed on vegetation, dig for roots and insects, or hunt small mammals. Grizzly bears make two seasonal migrations. They descend to the valley bottoms in the spring because these are the first areas to be free of snow. As areas higher up on the mountain become green, grizzly bears move up to these areas. By mid-summer, they descend again to the valley bottoms and lower valley walls where the berries tend to be most prevalent. When the berries fall off the bushes with the first frosts, grizzly bears move upslope again in search of roots, ground squirrels and other foods. By November, they begin denning. This usually occurs at elevations ranging from 6,000-7,000 feet / 1,800-2,100 meters.

Bears actively search for food in the fall in preparation for hibernation. Black and grizzly bears hibernate throughout the fall and winter making dens in hollow trees, caves and under fallen trees. Bears may awake during hibernation and search for food before returning to their dens.

During hibernation they rest in their dens and their heart rate drops from about 45 beats per minute to 10. Their hibernation period varies—about three to five months for black and grizzly bears, or up to seven months for polar bears and bears that live in northern Alaska.

ODORS AND FOOD SOURCES

Andy Russell, writing in *Grizzly Country*, tells a story that illustrates the grizzly's keen sense of smell. He describes how he once saw a grizzly crossing a valley and stopped to observe what would happen when the bear came upon his tracks. "He half reared, spun away, and broke into a tearing gallop for parts unknown," explains Russell. "Either I needed a bath worse than I thought, or that grizzly had some painful contact with men."

Bears' mucous membranes are about 100 times larger than those of people, and some researchers believe their sense of smell is better than that of dogs. Relative to body size, grizzly bears also have the largest brains of any carnivore. They can navigate by picking up scents on prevailing winds. Bears usually dodge people once they catch their scent: However, if the wind is in your face, be aware that it is harder for bears to catch your scent. Black bears can pick up a strong odor such as a dead animal from a distance of about a mile / 1.6 km. When the wind is blowing, they may detect campfire odors from about 2.5 miles / 4 km.

Black Bear Tracks

Animal carcasses and fish are two good food sources for bears and they pose a special risk for people. Since a dead animal is a highly concentrated food source, bears may feed on it for awhile, and then rest nearby. If people come across the carcass, a bear may think they are after its food and become aggressive. On the other hand, if a hunter kills an animal, bears may be drawn to him/her by the smell of blood.

While inland bears do not eat fish, coastal bears may be seen near shallow areas of lakes or streams. Tracks along the stream banks, trails through the bush, the remains of salmon or other fish, or overturned rocks indicate their presence. Coastal bears remember from year to year where to find the richest salmon runs and return to those areas because they are rich food sources.

AVOIDING BEAR ENCOUNTERS

• **WOMEN SHOULD TAKE PRECAUTIONS IF MENSTRUATING**: Although some researchers advise you to stay out of the backcountry at this time, studies do not conclusively show that your risk of bear attack increases. However, bears have an excellent sense of smell, and in a field study, polar bears detected the scent of menstruation about two thirds of the time. If you go into the backcountry while menstruating, use tampons instead of pads. If bear-resistant garbage bins are available, dispose of them there. If you are in the backcountry, burn them after use, or place them in plastic bags, seal them, and pack them out. Burying them is not a good idea: like garbage, bears may investigate, possibly causing problems for you or the next person in the area.

• **LEAVE POSTED AREAS:** If there is a problem bear or more bear activity than usual in a park, wardens and rangers may post a "Bear in Area" sign. When you see this sign, be cautious, get additional information and consider going to another area. If an aggressive bear is present, or if bears are feeding on a concentrated food source and should not be disturbed, trails are closed. Since signs and possibly the presence of flagging tape across trails indicate trail closures, a "do not disturb" is hard to miss but people do ignore them. In some parks, entering a closed area is an offense subject to fine.

• **KEEP DOGS ON LEASHES:** Dogs can easily anger a bear and if they fight, the dog will lose. In addition, if your dog is off its leash and meets a bear, it may run back to you with the bear in hot pursuit, endangering you as well as it. In Canada, it is against the law for dogs to spend a night in the backcountry in some national parks. In the United States, it is unlawful for pets to be present on trails in some areas even when leashed. Although it may seem unnecessary, dogs should be on leashes even at a drive-in campground.

• **USE A FLASHLIGHT AT NIGHT:** Since bears as well as many other animals are active at night, use a flashlight. This alerts animals to your presence and it helps you see if there is anything hiding in the bushes. If you hear a bear investigating your camp, be aware that it might stay in the area. If the bear obtained some food, it could stash it and rest nearby. If unsuccessful, it could try again.

• **TRAVEL IN GROUPS:** It is better to hike in groups of three or more rather than alone since you will probably make more noise; however, if you are alone make sure you are a noisy traveler. If children are with you, keep them within reach and possibly in-between adults. A group can generally deter a bear more easily than one person can.

Grizzly Bear
Tracks

B E A R S
(continued)

•ON THE TRAIL, WARN BEARS BY MAKING NOISE: Since bears may act aggressively if you surprise them, give them plenty of warning that you are around. Instead of relying on bear bells, which are fairly quiet, experts recommend you clap your hands. Or talk or sing loudly because the sound of your voice helps bears recognize you are human. On the other hand, it is also possible a young bear may hear the sound of your voice and become curious and investigate. Mountain bikers are generally at greater risk of startling a bear than hikers because of their speed and lack of noise.

• USE CAUTION NEAR RUSHING WATER OR DENSE VEGETATION: Be extra cautious near streams and dense vegetation since it masks sounds and bears may not hear you. People who work near rivers where their voices are muffled have found that a blast from a boat horn is effective in broadcasting their presence. Certain locations such as a bend in a trail or dense vegetation also conceal your presence.

Tips for Handling Defensive Bear Behavior

An interview with **Dr. Stephen Herrero,** a well-known North American expert on bears and author of *Bear Attacks: Their Causes and Avoidance.*

Defensive: a. serving to defend; resisting attack; n. the position of defending against attack. Defensively, adv. [L. *defendere,* to protect]–Webster's Dictionary

I was hiking in Valhalla Park, a remote mountainous area located in the Kootenays, British Columbia, just north of the state of Washington when I encountered a bear. Fighting my impulse to run, I spoke to the bear for a few minutes and then it dropped on all fours and ran off into the bush. How would you describe this type of bear encounter?

SH: It is very important to stress that about 99.9% of all interactions with bears are very peaceful ones—the bear goes the other way. In some situations the bear approaches you out of curiosity. In other cases, the bear gives a few aggressive displays and then backs off. These are all quite safe circumstances. I have been through hundreds if not thousands of them and many, many people I know have as well.

Why is talking to the bear in a low tone helpful in these situations?

SH: The bear is potentially agitated and afraid. Talking to the bear is wonderful, especially if you can do it in a nice level tone of voice because it helps to decrease the fear and potential aggression in the bear.

The bear might be afraid?

SH: In the typical encounter, the bear is quite agitated and to use a human term, "afraid." Because of uncertainty on the part of bears regarding what may happen, they sometimes attack defensively.

What is the best thing to do when a bear charges defensively at a person?

SH: The bear may be stopped by using bear spray. Our recent research suggests that bear spray may be as high as 80% effective in situations like that. However, it is still by far best to avoid these situations rather than try to thwart the bear during the situation.

How can the average person avoid a defensive encounter with a bear?

SH: By using all of the techniques which help you anticipate where bears are, and by making warning noises when you think there is a good probability that bears are near by. There are all sorts of things you can do to give the bears the option of not being surprised at close range.

What should you do if you do not have bear spray?

SH: If you do not have bear spray or if the bear spray fails, which it does sometimes, and you are attacked, then you are left with "playing dead" as a strategy to minimize injury. By playing dead—and especially by protecting your face and getting yourself face down on the ground—you will minimize injury.

• DO NOT REMAIN IN FEEDING AREAS OR WHERE BEARS MAY BE PRESENT: If you see indications a bear may be present, do not stay in the area. For example, a bear may eat up to 200,000 berries per day in the late summer and early fall, leaving behind berry-colored droppings. Do not dawdle in berry patches or other feeding areas. Other indications of the presence of bears are paw prints in mud or snow and partially buried carcasses. Since bears rub themselves against trees, they sometimes leave tufts of hair hanging from the bark and long horizontal claw marks on trees. Other signs of bear activity include crushed vegetation, overturned rocks and logs, or upturned earth where bears have been digging for roots or ground squirrels.

BEARS
(continued)

Tips for Handling Offensive Bear Behavior

Offensive: causing or giving offense; used in attack; insulting; unpleasant; n. attack; onset; aggressive action. [L. *offendere,* to strike against]–Webster's Dictionary

What is meant by "offensive behavior" on the part of the bear? Does it happen often?

SH: In an offensive situation, bears of both species—both black and grizzly bears—may treat a person as prey. Those incidents continue to be very, very rare. I have records dating from the turn of the century of about 40 incidents involving black bears and perhaps seven or eight involving grizzly bears.

How would the average person tell the difference between offensive and defensive behavior on the part of the bear?

SH: A bear will usually approach out of curiosity. And once it finds out what you are, it will back off. Sometimes, a bear continues to approach out of curiosity and this is a situation that you have to

manage carefully. By that I mean do not run from the bear and encourage it to push that curiosity further because there is sometimes a line when that curiosity can turn into aggressive curiosity.

What does a bear do when it is acting in an aggressive and offensive manner?

SH: Sometimes, the bear will have sized up the situation and decide to make a rush and attack offensively without a lot of preliminary build-up. Typically, the offensive attacks do not have any of the aggressive displays associated with defensive attacks; they do not have bluff charges, they do not have snorting or blowing and they do not have any vocalization associated with them.

Instead of acting in defense of its young or its space, and making bluff charges against the person, the bear deliberately attacks the person?

SH: Offensive behavior involves simply a stalking and attacking on the part of the bear. Again, I want to stress just how extremely rare

these things are. They are real but they are extremely rare. We probably have at least 700,000 black bears in North America and perhaps 70,000 grizzly and brown bears. So having a predacious incident or a few predaceous incidents from all those bears in all of those years, really it is not very much.

What is your best means of protecting yourself when the bear is treating you as something to eat for dinner?

SH: In an offensive situation, where the bear is acting offensively, you do not play dead. That simply encourages the worst case scenario, which is to encourage the bear's aggression. And so regardless of whether it might be a grizzly bear or black bear, you must fight back and try to deter the bear. Now that is best done either with weapons, bear spray or as a group. One person can potentially deter a bear but they just have to be that much more aggressive and capable than a group of four or five people.

Bear Repellent Study: Pepper Spray

What is pepper spray?

Pepper spray contains an ingredient called capsaicin (trans-8-methyl-N-vanillyn-6-nonenamide) that is found in a number of plants including cayenne peppers. Oleoresin capsaicin (often called OC spray) irritates sensory nerve endings causing temporary pain.

How effective is it?

Researchers have studied the effectiveness of OC spray on both caged and free-ranging black and grizzly bears. Generally speaking, when bears are sprayed directly in the face, they blink their eyes, stop their previous behavior, retreat and rub their eyes. Some bears may approach again, and may have to be sprayed a number of times.

The information below summarizes the researchers' findings. from a report, *Field Use of Capsicum Spray as a Bear Deterrent.* Researchers advise that "results should be viewed with caution given the lack of controlled methodology."

To be effective, pepper spray must contact the bear's eyes.

• **Aggressive brown/grizzly bears:** In 15 out of 16 cases, the bears stopped their behavior after being sprayed. Six of the bears continued to act aggressively. Three of them attacked the sprayer, although one bear stopped and left after being sprayed again. Two of these cases involved a sow with cubs.

• **Aggressive black bears:** These cases include sudden encounters and possible predation. In four out of four cases, the bears stopped their behavior but did not leave the area.

• **Curious or food-seeking brown/grizzly bears:** In 20 out of 20 cases, the bears stopped their behavior; 18 left the area.

• **Curious or food-seeking black bears:** In 19 out of 26 cases, the bears stopped their behavior; 14 of them left the area, and six of the 14 returned. Although the number of aggressive black bears studied was small, their study suggests that OC may be less effective against aggressive black bears than aggressive brown/grizzly bears. It is unknown whether OC spray would deter a predaceous black bear.

What affects the operation of OC sprays?

Pepper sprays do not always operate perfectly. Problems may arise either from mechanical failure or from their concentration or range.

Bear Repellent Study: Pepper Spray

• **Mechanical problems:** Pressure loss has resulted in spray dribbling down the side of the can rather than dispersing in a mist. The spray has shot out in a stream rather than a mist. Failures have also occurred due to abuse; handles have broken off rendering deployment impossible. In another incident, the sprayer pressed the deployment mechanism and the entire can shot off.

• **Operational difficulties:** Some OC sprays have a safety device to prevent accidental deployment. You must remove it before spraying. Before buying a pepper spray, consider the following questions: Do you intend to carry the spray in a holster? Can you get at it easily? Will it catch on bushes or other objects? How does your spray operate? Can you get at the trigger easily?

• **Concentration and range:** OC sprays have different concentrations of capsaicin, the active ingredient, ranging from one to 10%. Higher concentrations may result in a longer recovery period. The range, which is determined by the type of propellant used, also varies from about 16-23 feet / 5-7 meters. Propellants used for OC sprays in Canada are different from those used in the United States.

• **Environment:** Head winds or crosswinds interfere with the range of the spray. Heavy rain and dense bush can also disperse it.

TIPS FOR USING PEPPER SPRAY

• **Try to use at close range:** If you find yourself in a situation where you must use OC spray against an aggressive or curious bear, remember the spray is most efficient at close range and that it must contact the eyes of the bear.

• **Try to spray downwind:** If the wind is blowing in your direction, the spray may miss the bear, and even worse, blow back in your face. It may render you incapable of either playing dead or fighting back.

• **Do not move toward the bear:** If you advance, the bear may interpret your behavior as aggressive. Wait until it comes within your range.

• **Spray toward the face:** Since OC spray disperses as a cloud, rather than a stream, you don't have to shoot with pinpoint accuracy. However, the spray must contact the bear's eyes to be effective.

• **Leave the area after spraying:** Move away to prevent any of the spray contacting you. Even if the spray successfully repels the bear, there is no guarantee the bear won't return so it is best to leave the area.

TREATING A PERSON WHO HAS BEEN PEPPER SPRAYED

Although being sprayed with OC spray is painful, it does not cause any long-term damage. Most people react by closing their eyes and temporarily lose some muscle coordination. If someone is accidentally sprayed, get him or her out of the mist and into fresh air. Then treat for specific irritation to the eyes or skin. The information below provides suggestions for immediate first aid; however, you may need to seek medical attention if the inflammation is severe.

• **Eyes:** Getting OC spray in your eyes causes an inflammation at the superficial level of the cornea. It generally heals within a day. To treat, flush the eyes with water for up to 20 minutes. If you wear contacts, remove them since irritants may get trapped behind or in them. Give them a thorough cleaning to remove any contaminants. You may have to discard the lenses.

• **Skin:** Wash the skin with soap and water or with alcohol to remove irritants. Bathing the irritated area in vinegar solution (5% acetic acid) decreases pain even if you do it up to half an hour after contact. You can continue this for as long as necessary. A severe irritation may require several hours of bathing. If problems continue, see a doctor or call a poison center.

• **Lungs or stomach:** Inhaling OC spray may severely irritate your stomach or lungs. If this occurs, see a doctor.

B E A R S
(continued)

CAMPING IN BEAR COUNTRY

• **COMMERCIAL CAMPGROUNDS AREN'T NECESSARILY BEAR-PROOF; BE AWARE:** When you stay in a commercial or drive-in campground, there is a tendency to think that you must be safe, especially since there are so many other people around. But this is not always true. For example, a grizzly sow and cub in a campground at Lake Louise, Canada, attacked six campers one summer, and four were seriously injured.

• **CHECK FOR FOOD REMNANTS:** Check your potential campsite to make sure there is nothing nearby that might attract a bear such as an animal carcass. Have other people camped there before you, and if so, did they keep a clean camp or have they created a problem for you? Are there lots of squirrels and other small animals around begging for food? If there is a metal fire-pit, are food remnants buried in the ashes? Check whether there are any recent bear signs such as claw marks in trees, scat, tracks, or holes where bears have dug for roots or rodents.

• **CAMP AWAY FROM ANIMAL TRAILS, THICK BRUSH, FOOD SOURCES AND RUNNING WATER:** Choose a site that is well away from areas that bears might frequent. Since bears, like people, use trails, camp at least 350 feet / 100 meters away from animal trails. Keep away from streams since bears may fish along the banks. Bears also use rivers as traveling routes, so pitching a tent on a riverbank might be scenic but not too safe. In addition, the sound of rushing water masks your presence. Make sure you are not setting up camp in a lush berry patch or other food source.

• **USE THE TRIANGLE SYSTEM OF EATING, SLEEPING AND STORAGE:** When you are in the backcountry, separate your sleeping, cooking, and storage areas. Locate your cooking and storage areas 350 feet / 100 meters away from your sleeping area. Try to situate your cooking area so food odors do not drift down to your sleeping area. This decreases the chances of a bear smelling food and stumbling upon you in its search. In addition, try to have a clear line of sight from your sleeping area to your cooking and storage areas. This gives you a better chance of seeing what might be happening as well as more time to react.

Make sure you do not eat, cook, or store food or smelly substances in your tent. Avoid getting food odors on your clothing, sleeping bag, or tent. If your clothes are full of food odors, sleep in different clothing, and store your smelly clothes with your food.

• **PLACE YOUR TENTS IN EITHER A SEMI-CIRCLE OR A STRAIGHT LINE:** Using a tent is safer than sleeping in the open. However, if you are tenting in a group, do not place all of your tents in a circle. If a bear stumbles into your camp at night, it may get confused and caught in the middle of your tents. Arranging tents in a semi-circle or straight line, giving a frightened bear a clear escape route.

• **COOK FOODS WITHOUT STRONG ODORS:** Since bears have an excellent sense of smell, cooking foods such as bacon broadcasts your presence. Bring powdered foods, pasta, or freeze-dried foods instead. In addition, bears are attracted to toiletry items such as shaving cream, toothpast and soap. If you fish, be aware that the smell of fish strongly attracts bears. Wash your hands thoroughly and try to eliminate fish odors from your clothing. Rid fish offal along stream banks in fast running wate or the depths of a lake.

• **DISPOSE OF YOUR GARBAGE APPROPRIATELY:** As soon as you have finished eating, wash your dishes and store them in a bear-proof location. When washing up, strain the dishwater to isolate particles of food and place them with the garbage. Dispose of wastewater in provided areas. If there are none, make sure you dispose of it at least 350 feet / 100 meters away from your sleeping area. Leaving garbage around your campsite may attract bears and create problems for the next campers. Do not burn it or bury it. Place garbage in plastic bags and carry it out. Avoid putting garbage in out-houses, as bears may be attracted to them, and therefore people.

B E A R S
(continued)

CAMPING IN BEAR COUNTRY

1. Place your tent on a small rise so food odors do not drift down to it. Separate your sleeping, cooking, and storage areas using the triangle system.

2. Store your food by suspending it above the ground or use bear proof storage containers. Do not store food or any smelly substance in your tent.

3. Camp well away from animal trails since bears may use these at night.

4. Camp well away from rivers. Bears may fish there or travel along the banks.

5. Camp well away from food sources as these may attract bears. Check for food remnants, garbage or carcasses and avoid areas having these.

B

BEARS
(continued)

• **STORE YOUR FOOD APPROPRIATELY:** If you are in a drive-in campground, do not leave your food and garbage out on a picnic table where bears can easily reach it. Coolers are not bear-resistant either. Leaving food in a tent is also unsafe since bears can easily rip through nylon and may endanger you in an attempt to get at your food. Your best approach is to store food and garbage in the trunk of your vehicle, although bears can be aggressive and could damage your vehicle. Some campgrounds have bear-proof storage and garbage facilities. If there are bear-proof containers provided, make sure you store all of your food and any other odorous substances there. This includes toothpaste, hand creams and pet food.

If these caches are not available put your food in plastic bags and seal them tightly. This decreases food odors. Then put your plastic bags in a large stuff sack. Suspend the stuff sack from two trees and make sure it is at least 15 feet / 4.5 meters off the ground and about 4.5 feet / 1.5 meters away from the top and side supports. Some campsites have cables for this purpose. You attach your food bag to a cable, hoist it off the ground, and then secure the cable. However, since pulleys may not be available, carry your own rope and pulley system for hanging food in the backcountry.

Black Bear Profile

Grizzly Bear Profile

If you cannot hang your food from trees, suspend it from a bridge, or over a rock face. Use whatever feature is available to ensure that a bear cannot get at it. Since bears are curious animals, and may investigate any object in your campsite such as your pack, you might consider hanging anything that you do not want a bear to chew up.

Above treeline, adequate food-hanging trees are not always handy. In situations like this, store your food in bear resistant containers and stash them at least 600 feet / 200 meters downwind or downslope from your camp. If they are sealed properly, bears should not be able to detect odors. Bear canisters also keep food secure from other animals such as raccoons, cougars, and rodents. Bear canisters are mandatory in some parks.

AVOIDING BEAR ENCOUNTERS

Although meeting a bear may be frightening, remember there are hundreds of encounters every year, most of which do not result in injury. Stay calm and take a moment to assess your situation. Consider whether it is a grizzly or a black bear. Grizzly bears are more aggressive than black bears. However, grizzlies rarely climb trees while black bears routinely do so. Since bears are unpredictable, and have different personalities, no one can be certain how a bear will react. However, the suggestions below are based on current knowledge of bear behavior and may increase your margin of safety.

B E A R S
(continued)

• **IF YOU SEE A BEAR IN THE DISTANCE AND IT DOES NOT SEE YOU, SLOWLY BACK AWAY, LEAVING THE AREA THE WAY YOU CAME:** If you can, leave when the bear has its head down so it does not notice you. After you leave, travel upwind so it can pick up your scent. Even if the bear is some distance away, treat the situation cautiously. The distance between you and the bear could shorten dramatically if the bear chose to run in your direction. A grizzly bear can run 66% faster than the fastest human and bears also run downhill.

• **ALTHOUGH YOU MIGHT WANT TO OBSERVE THE BEAR MORE CLOSELY, DO NOT:** Since you cannot judge how close you can get before you will aggravate the bear, the safest option is to give it a lot of room.

• **IF YOU SEE A BEAR IN THE DISTANCE AND IT HAS NOT SEEN YOU BUT IS MOVING TOWARDS YOU:** Slowly back away. Get away from its traveling route. If you are on a path, get off it and give the bear enough room to get around you. If you cannot get completely away and you think that it will notice you soon, warn it you are there. Talking in low tones may help the bear identify you as human. Although it is useful to make noise, do not shout, since this may startle it.

• **IF YOU SEE A BEAR WITH CUBS AT ANY DISTANCE, LEAVE THE AREA IMMEDIATELY:** A mother bear, especially a grizzly, will aggressively defend her cubs at the slightest provocation. If you see a cub but not a mother bear, be aware the mother will be nearby. However, she may react by coming to her cub, rather than charging you.

• **IF A BEAR SEES YOU AND STARTS TO FOLLOW YOU, SLOWLY BACK AWAY:** Resist the impulse to run; you cannot outrun the bear, and many animals naturally chase after an animal that runs. If the bear continues to follow you, distract it by leaving a piece of equipment or your pack on the ground. Try not to leave food since this may cause the bear to come after you, in search of more. In addition, if the bear associates people with food, it can cause problems for other people as well as the bear.

Climbing a tree is useful if it is a grizzly bear and if you can quickly get at least 12 feet / 4 meters off the ground. Climbing a tree might give you a bit of an advantage even if it's a black bear since you will be in a good position to grab a branch or other object and fight it off.

• **IF YOU SURPRISE A BEAR AT CLOSE RANGE, DO NOT RUN:** Instead, talk in low tones, wave your arms and try to help it identify you as human. Stand your ground or back away slowly. Try to get upwind of the bear. If the bear stands on its hind legs with its nose in the air, it is trying to get your scent or see you more clearly. However, if the bear makes a "whoofing" sound, puts its head down, snaps its jaws together, and puts its ears back, it is angry. Bears attack by running on all four legs.

*"Climb the mountains and get their good tidings.
Nature's peace will flow into you
As sunshine flows into trees.
The winds will blow their own freshness into you,
And storms their energy ..."*

— John Muir

B E A R S
(continued)

BIGHORN SHEEP

BIGHORN SHEEP

Unlike deer and elk, which are members of the deer family, bighorn sheep belong to the bovid family. Bighorn sheep are smaller than elk and mule deer but stockier. Males weigh about 300 pounds / 130 kilograms while females weigh about 200 pounds / 90 kilograms.

Because of their smaller size, people may mistake ewes and lambs for Rocky Mountain goats; however, the horns of the goats are straighter and black in color. Unlike Rocky Mountain goats, which are white, bighorn sheep are mostly light brown in color with a white patch on their rump and a short brown tail. While elk and mule deer have branching antlers, bighorn sheep have horns. Although both sexes have horns, the horns of the rams are longer and heavier. The horns grow in a spiral that may reach 360 degrees.

While elk and deer shed grow their antlers each year, bighorn sheep retain their horns throughout their lives and grow them continuously except for a short period during the winter. Researchers believe daylight may be a factor in the growth of horns. Unlike elk, whose age cannot be determined by the size of the antlers, the age of a bighorn sheep can be estimated by counting the rings or year marks on its horns.

Bighorn sheep are well known for their butting contests, which occur during the autumn rutting season as the rams fight for superiority. Although both rams and ewes engage in butting in order to establish dominance, butting contests between rams may lead to actual battles. The rams back off, rear up on their hind legs, and then charge forward, butting their horns and making a loud ringing sound, sometimes breaking the tips of their horns. The winner achieves the right to mate with a certain ewe. Bighorn sheep mate in the late fall and the lambs are born in the spring. Soon after birth, the lambs negotiate the steep terrain along with the adults.

Grazing animals, bighorn sheep feed primarily on grasses, forbs, and sedges in the summer and grasses and shrubbery in the winter. Once common in western North America, bighorn sheep lost most of their range due to competition with domestic livestock for food, disease acquired from domestic sheep, and excessive hunting. In the northwest United States, bighorn sheep have been reintroduced extensively. Bighorn sheep are found in mountainous areas at any elevation. These animals favor steep rocky slopes near open areas.

BIGHORN SHEEP AND PEOPLE

Similar to elk and mule deer, bighorn sheep generally shy away from people in a wilderness setting. However, bighorn sheep that live in parks or near towns become habituated to people and lose their natural wariness.

In the spring, bighorn sheep are plagued by parasites such as ticks, which can carry diseases such as Rocky Mountain Spotted Fever. Ticks are often prevalent in areas that sheep frequent. Bighorn sheep can also carry a disease called contagious ecthyma or soremouth, a contagious viral disease that produces lesions in the mouth, nose and gums. When a person feeds an infected sheep, the sheep can pass the disease by contacting or licking the hands.

Again, similar to elk and mule deer, bighorn sheep are at their most aggressive during the autumn rutting season and have chased people. They have also been known to damage vehicles. Bighorn sheep that seek food from people

Bighorn sheep are most aggressive during the autumn rut and spring calving seasons.

along trails or in vehicles can become aggressive. They can approach people seeking food. The herd may end up crowding children and adults or react as a group and cause fear and a potential human/wildlife conflict. Rams can become quite determined to get food and can react defensively if threatened.

In some mountainous areas, bighorn sheep are habituated to road salt. It is difficult to dehabituate the sheep since the salt is readily available. Unfortunately, the tendency of bighorn sheep to wander onto the roads causes "sheep jams" as they block lanes and stopped vehicles stack up. This also results in accidents that damage vehicles and injure or kill wildlife.

AVOIDING ENCOUNTERS WITH BIGHORN SHEEP

Do not feed bighorn sheep. Since bighorn sheep may pass diseases or parasites on to people, the best defense is to avoid close contact and resist the impulse to feed them by hand. If people stop feeding them, they will also be less likely to aggressively seek food from hikers or people in vehicles. This will decrease the number of combative incidents and road jams.

BISON

Give bison plenty of space since they can get aggressive if approached.

BISON

A member of the cow family, bison are immense in size: males weigh some 1,500 pounds / 900 kilograms, while females weigh about 1,300 pounds / 600 kilograms. These shaggy creatures are the largest land animals in North America. Bison are easy to identify by their dark brown color, prominent shoulder hump and massive head. Although both sexes have black upturned horns, the male's horns are larger. Bison do not shed their horns.

Although the correct appellation for these large shaggy creatures is "bison," many people refer to these massive animals as buffalo. They were once widespread throughout western North America and ranged throughout grasslands and mountain meadows. However, bison populations were decimated by the late 1900s, primarily because of over hunting. Bison are now found in pockets throughout North America and exist primarily in national and state parks. In Canada, for example, bison are found in Banff and Jasper national parks. In the United States, bison have been reintroduced to Yellowstone National Park among other areas. Small herds also exist on private ranches. For many people, bison are a symbol of the American West.

Males and females are found in separate herds except for the summer rutting season. At this time, the males compete for the harem by knocking their heads against each other. Males are especially ill tempered at this time. The calves are born in the spring and are reddish in color. Cows are quite protective of their calves and may respond to threats by charging. Although their usual pace is a walk, bison can sometimes lope and these large animals gallop when they stampede.

AVOIDING ENCOUNTERS WITH BISON

In parks, bison are often separated from people by the use of paddocks. Where bison roam freely, however, make sure you stay at least 500 feet / 150 meters away from these wild animals. Bison are unpredictable and can become aggressive if approached or if a dog is nearby.

BUFFALO

See BISON.

BUFFALO

BUSH
TERRAIN

BUSH TERRAIN

Most people do not choose to tackle bush terrain. However, it may be necessary from time to time because trails in the backcountry change due to natural or human processes. A faint trail can become overgrown by a dense thicket of shrubs and grasses. Rockfall may obscure part of a trail and as you pick your way across the rubble, you cannot find your trail as you reach the other side. Trails may be blocked by snow necessitating a detour, or rain or streams may wash out sections. When following a faint or braided trail, it is easy to let your mind wander for a few moments only to find that the faint trail has now disappeared into nothing. The same thing can occur on blazed trails.

People did not originally make most of the trails in the backcountry. They were old animal trails, or trails leading to a favorite fishing spot. You may find that the trail you are following does not lead you where you thought it was going. Past or present logging or mining practices can also change or obscure the trail.

The nature of the trail also changes depending on climate. On the West Coast, for example, where there is abundant rainfall, the undergrowth is lush. Farther inland, where the climate is continental, the vegetation changes and species adapted to drier conditions thrive.

What kinds of challenges are found in thick brush? It is generally much more difficult to travel through dense undergrowth than a trail, however faint. The wind may have caused old trees to blow down into a jumble of partially decayed logs. Rocks entangled in the shrubs offer unstable footing, and wet or shaded areas may be slippery.

Thick brush may obscure difficult terrain such as cliffs. The thin branches offer feeble handholds. When shrubs and trees such as alders grow on an angle, it is easy to slip and twist an ankle. Plants such as poison ivy may be present to add to your woes. Moss may obscure small depressions in the ground or patches of unstable rock.

When it rains, travel becomes even more difficult because everything becomes very slick. Unstable boulders now have a thin film of water over them to make footing slippery. The ground, entangled with shrubs, becomes muddy. Branches that whip back in your face now have the added insult of droplets of rain. The whole environment becomes very wet as you encounter rain falling from the sky, water dripping off branches, and water oozing through openings in the undergrowth.

It is easy to get separated from your friends in dense brush because it obscures visibility. Also, the members of your group—each determined to find the trail, a trail, any trail—may tend to wander off in their search. It is also difficult to hear your friends when you become separated in dense brush because it muffles sounds.

The other possible hazard that awaits you in dense brush is startling animals. You may not see them until you are upon them. Insects tend to thrive in dense brush, and some of them enjoy wet or marshy areas in particular. Reptiles may also make their home in thick undergrowth.

Avalanche tracks also present challenges. When the snow slides in the winter, it takes trees, shrubs, rocks and other debris with it. A jumble of debris is deposited at the bottom of the path. Snow may be tucked within the boulders and cause them to become slippery. Patches of snow may also be present in shady places and especially along narrow creek beds.

BUSH
TERRAIN
(continued)

ROUTE FINDING IN DIFFICULT BUSH

One of the best ways to deal with some of the terrors of thick brush is to attempt to avoid it altogether. If you find your trail has faded, backtrack until you can find it again. Once you have found it, try the trail again, this time concentrating on staying on "the" trail, if there is one. If the trail does indeed entirely fade out, consider retracing your steps to your original starting point. Even a faint animal trail makes for easier traveling than no trail. However, be aware that animal trails may not lead you where you want to go. They take you where they want to go.

One of the other options is simply to find a higher route. Depending on the difficulty of the terrain, climb high above the valley to treeline. Travel in the alpine until you find an easy way to descend back to your original route.

If you do not want to go as high as treeline, consider using spurs or buttresses above the valley instead. These may offer a straightforward line of travel and allow you to escape from the rigors of the brush altogether. Ridges and buttresses also offer a good view of the surrounding valley, which will help you to see your way.

Alternatively, go slightly higher than the brush in the valley and look for patches of snow. Lingering snowfields and snowslopes may offer a much easier route than dense brush if conditions are good. Early in the season, the snow may be firm and offer solid footing. Later on, snow patches may melt and become a tangle of slush. Another possibility is to travel on scree above the brush, if scree slopes are available. Traversing scree is strenuous but it may less strenuous than the brush in the valley. The occasional patch of snow may be present on scree.

If you encounter avalanche debris, also consider selecting a route slightly above it. There may be less debris higher on the slope. However, areas cleared of trees may have dense undergrowth of alders and willows. Another option is to go even higher in search of open grassy slopes. These may enable you to bypass all of the brush altogether. However, keep in mind that bears enjoy feeding on avalanche slopes in the spring. They look for winterkill among the debris and feed on the bulbs of glacier lilies, which grow along the sides of the snow.

Instead of going high to avoid the brush, you may also consider traveling low. There may be animal trails near water. Streambeds can offer a relatively straightforward route. If they are shallow or dry, it may be easier to descend directly down the stream instead of walking along the banks. However, water takes the easiest line downwards and this could involve descending over slippery rock bands. Streams are also definite features on the landscape. If you are concerned about getting lost in the brush, a streambed has the advantage of providing a distinct route. Streams are usually shown on topographical maps.

If you do choose to go through the brush, try to find a route in the densest timber. Shade provided by the trees inhibits the growth of an impenetrable understory. Dense timber will offer an easier route than thick low brush.

TIPS FOR HANDLING DIFFICULT BUSH

• **DRESS PROTECTIVELY:** If you are in for a bit of bushwhacking put on a layers of clothing such as pants, a shirt or jacket and a hat. If it starts to rain put on raingear right away.

"I heard trees falling for hours at the rate of one every two or three minutes; some uprooted, partly on account of the loose, water-soaked condition of the ground; others broken straight across, where some weakness caused by fire had determined the spot."

—John Muir

Taking a trail is usually faster and more enjoyable than trudging through difficult bush.

• **TRAVEL CLOSELY TOGETHER TO AVOID GETTING SEPARATED:** Be in sight or in calling distance of your companions at all times. Call to each other routinely so that you can be sure all keep on track. Carry a whistle as dense brush obscures sound. However, do not travel so closely together that branches whipping backward could strike the person behind.

• **TAKE YOUR TIME AND HAVE PATIENCE WHILE TRAVELING IN THE BRUSH:** Bushwhacking can be both physically and mentally exhausting. If you rush around, you are more likely to get lost or to stumble and injure yourself. Call out often to warn animals of your presence.

• **CARRY A MAP AND COMPASS AND KNOW HOW TO USE IT:** When you travel in dense brush, you are by definition off a defined trail and it is easy to lose your way. In preparation for potential thrashes in the bush, learn more about the mountain range in which you are traveling. Each has its own distinct patterns of terrain and vegetation. By becoming familiar with the area, you will be better able to make informed route finding choices.

BUSH
TERRAIN
(continued)

Getting Hurt in the Mountains:

An interview with Chic Scott, backcountry skier, mountain adventurer and guide book writer of *Ski Trails in the Canadian Rockies, Summits and Icefields,* as well as *Pushing the Limits: The Story of Canadian Mountaineering.*

Who is responsible when someone gets injured or killed in the mountains?

CS: Well, you have to be the one who takes responsibility for yourself. If you find yourself in a hospital bed, injured after an accident, it does no good to blame somebody else. You are the one who is hurt, and sure you may be able to sue someone else and get compensation, but your life may be ruined.

You need to take responsibilty for yourself?

CS: Mountaineering is not a spectator sport. You participate in all aspects of it. Mountaineering is also about accepting responsibility for your own decisions. We live in a world where we do little for ourselves anymore except wash the dishes and buy the groceries. Professionals marry us, bury us, and take our appendixes out. It is refreshing to go into the mountains and leave the cell phone behind. If something happens, if the weather turns or somebody sprains an ankle, you must rely on yourself. You cannot just phone 911 and expect that somebody is going to come to your aid.

How can you learn to take responsibility for yourself when you are new to the mountains?

CS: Right from the very beginning, you should sometimes lead your own trips. They do not have to be difficult, and in fact they should not be if your experience level is low. But you should conceive of the trip, organize it, and execute it yourself. It may just be hiking along the river valley in a local park in your city, but that is fine; it is a place to start. And then as you gradually develop more skills and more confidence, then your expeditions can become more difficult. It is a far greater achievement I think to climb a modest mountain making your own decisions under your own leadership than to be dragged up Mount Everest as many people are nowadays.

What about relying on others who are more experienced in the mountains than you are?

CS: If you decide to go with a friend or an amateur leader, then you must really be very careful. Take a situation where, for example, the boyfriend wants to take the girlfriend out and show her how to climb. Often, the boyfriend wants to impress the girlfriend. It is more of an ego thing than a desire to show her a nice day out in the mountains. A lot of accidents also happen from poor leadership—the leader gets people into situations beyond their abilities. If you hire a guide, you are not relying on a guide to make all the decisions because

Chic Scott

you made the decision in the first place to hire a guide. Then, you should still watch the guide with a critical eye so you never relinquish your own decision-making ability. Hiring a guide does not mean you turn off all decision-making and all critical faculties.

What should motivate people to go to the mountains?

CS: For many of us, mountaineering is about overcoming your ego and your vanity and your ambition. Mountains are never conquered. If the weather is good, and the snow conditions are good, and your body is working fine, then maybe you will climb your peak. But all it takes is a little change in the weather and the mountain will tell you who is boss. In the mountains, it is unhealthy to let your ego drive you.

When I interviewed 90 of the leading mountaineers in Canada for my book on the history of mountaineering, very few expressed any sense they were climbing for ego or ambition. Some of them said the relation-

Whose Fault Is It?

People must take responsiblity for their own personal safety while traveling in the mountains.

ships they formed with others was most important and others said the relationships they formed with Nature was most important. They all felt the challenge was important—the physical challenge, the mental challenge. But none of them seemed to indicate that ticking off a list of ascents or trophy hunting was part of that.

Sometimes it might even take more mental and physical strength to turn back than to make an ascent?

CS: Often it is harder to turn around than to keep going. You can say it takes more courage. Often, you are so into what you are doing, and your adrenaline level is so high that courage does not exist any more. You are not afraid. You are just completely involved, and your whole body is exhilarated. This is what sometimes happens in the Himalayas, for example, where you push so hard for the summit—often it takes years and years just to get there—so when you want to turn back, you cannot, you keep going and cannot stop. It takes a real conscious effort just to grab that upward momentum and turn it into a downward momentum.

I guess that sometimes people do not realize the danger they are in.

CS: Some people do not know the difference between "real" danger and "pretend" danger. These days, kids see movies such as *Cliffhanger*—where the hero falls into a freezing river full of ice with only his T-shirt on, and he comes out, and he is not frozen. Some kids do not know the difference between real danger and pretend danger. So they go snowboarding in the backcountry, and they are not really aware that the danger is very real and very serious. You must learn to be careful and respect the mountains right from day one.

C

CORNICES
See SNOW-COVERED TERRAIN

COUGARS
See MOUNTAIN LIONS

COYOTES

Coyotes are a member of the family *Canidae* that includes dogs, wolves and foxes. The coyote is classified as *Canis latrans* which means "barking dog." The name "coyote" is derived from the Aztec word *coyotl*. In that society, coyote was venerated: the moon goddess was named Coyolxauhqui and the hunting god, Coyotlinauatl.

Resembling a fox with its sharp, pointed ears and long muzzle, a coyote varies in color but is often gray on the backside and brown along the sides. Coyotes are about one-third smaller than wolves and have bushier tails. Unlike the wolf, which carries its tail straight when it runs, the coyote carries its tail low. While females are generally smaller than males, an adult weighs about 20-25 pounds / 9-11 kilograms. From the tip of their noses to the end of their bushy black-tipped tails, coyotes are about five feet / 1.5 meters long.

Coyotes rely on their exceptional sight, hearing, and smell to locate and hunt small prey such as mice and rabbits. Their diet changes with the season. In the summer, their diet includes plants, fawns, and small rodents such as meadow voles. In the winter, they eat larger prey such as snowshoe hare, carrion, and sometimes deer. Although active at dawn and dusk, they are most active at night. Their daytime activity increases when mating or rearing pups since their food requirements are greater.

Coyotes generally hunt alone or in pairs. About 70% of the time, they are successful in catching small rodents such as mice by pouncing on them with their front feet. When they pursue small, fleet-footed animals such as rabbits, coyotes can travel at 35 MPH / 56 km/hr. Unlike a dog, which tends to wander, a coyote's track is straight since it places each hind paw exactly in the forepaw's print.

COYOTES AND PEOPLE

Although coyotes are predators, they do not generally prey on people. Coyotes have bitten people and inflicted wounds but there are no documented records of fatal attacks. A few aggressive incidents have occurred, but these incidents are not normal behavior for coyotes. These are isolated incidents where a coyote crossed the line between being habituated and trying to acquire food. When coyotes become used to people, they lose their fear and connect people with food.

Coyotes can get aggressive if you invade their space. If you get too close, you put yourself at risk for a minor injury. You may also put their pups at risk. If people disturb their den, coyotes may abandon it.

The most alarming stories about coyotes involve children. Again, these incidents are highly unusual. In Canada, coyotes attacked some children in the mountain resort town of Jasper on two separate occasions. These events were predatory—the children were small, pre-school aged and they were attacked in their yards.

Apparently, the coyotes became aggressive because of a high coyote population and a decline in their regular food source. The incident occurred during winter when a heavy snowfall made hunting more difficult. The coyotes, under the stress of inadequate food, became bold and ventured into the town site. The small children, playing outside in the yard, may have resembled prey.

Similar to wolves, coyotes can be antagonistic to dogs. One coyote lures a dog away, and then a small pack kills the dog. Coyotes also mate with dogs resulting in a hybrid known as a coydog.

AVOIDING ENCOUNTERS WITH COYOTES

• Since coyotes can become aggressive if you get too close, especially if they have a den nearby, give them their space. Watch them from a distance. If you think you may be invading their space, back away slowly. Do not run since this invites the coyote to chase you.

• If a coyote is acting aggressively to you in a close encounter, be aggressive. Grab a stick and defend yourself. The coyote will probably run off.

• Since coyote/dog encounters occur, keep your dog on a leash. This reduces the possibility of your dog fighting a losing battle with a small pack of coyotes or running back to you for help.

• Although the chance of a coyote preying on your small children is rare, avoid letting them play alone in the backcountry. Monitor them closely and make sure larger children or adults are nearby.

• Show your children pictures of coyotes. Without scaring them, make them aware of potential hazards and how to handle encounters.

COYOTES
(continued)

[The coyote]
"has a general
slinking expres-
sion all over.
The coyote, is a
living, breath-
ing allegory of
Want."

—Mark Twain

CRYPTOSPORIDIUM

CRYPTOSPORIDIUM

Cryptosporidium, a word that means "hidden spore," is a single-celled protozoan. Scientists have identified four species of the protozoan including C. parvum, which can cause an gastro-intestinal disease called cryptosporidosis in humans. The disease generally develops about eight to ten days after ingestion of the oocysts (an egg-like form of the parasite that causes infection). Some people have oocysts in their stool but have no symptoms of the disease. Healthy people can experience symptoms such as stomach cramps, watery diarrhea and headaches but usually recover on their own in about two weeks.

However, cryptosporidosis can become much more severe in people with suppressed immune systems. The disease can cause symptoms such as weight loss and dehydration and can even become life threatening. Among others, people who are on therapies that suppress the immune system, who are HIV-positive or who are undergoing chemotherapy should exercise special caution about contracting cryptosporidosis.

HOW DO PEOPLE GET CRYPTOSPORIDIUM?

People can get cryptosporidium by ingesting something, such as water, which is contaminated with the parasite. The oocyst is excreted in the feces of infected animals and people. Because of surface run-off, the water in mountain lakes, rivers, and streams, often contain the parasite. In one study, 77 out of 107 water samples, collected from untreated surface water in six western states, tested positive for the parasite. It is not usually found in ground water because of natural soil filtration.

People can also get cryptosporidium by eating raw or undercooked fruits and vegetables that have been washed in contaminated water, or have contacted contaminated soil or feces. The parasite can also be present on environmental surfaces that are contaminated by minute portions of the infected stool. In addition, cryptosporidium can be transferred through direct person-to-person contact or animal to person. The potential for waterborne transmission of cryptosporidium is thought to be as great or greater than giardia. It is also thought to have more potential for animal to human transmission than giardia. Cryptoposporidium is smaller than giardia and more resistant to disinfectants.

AVOIDING / MANAGING CRYPTOSPORIDIUM

• **AVOID DRINKING WATER DIRECTLY FROM MOUNTAIN LAKES, RIVERS, AND STREAMS, SINCE THE PARASITE IS OFTEN PRESENT IN THE WATER:** Instead, boil water intended for drinking for one full minute. Store it in a clean, sealed water bottle, and avoid touching the inside of the bottle.

• **DRINK BOTTLED WATER THAT HAS BEEN TREATED FOR CRYPTOSPORIDIUM:** This includes distilled water, water treated by reverse osmosis, or filtered with a micron size of 0.5 or smaller. This size is smaller than that used to filter giardia. Chlorine is not effective in destroying cryptosporidium, but research shows ozone might be useful.

• **WASH FRUIT AND VEGETABLES THAT WILL BE EATEN RAW WITH WATER TREATED FOR CRYPTOSPORIDIUM:** Peeling fruit will increase the margin of safety.

• **WASH HANDS FREQUENTLY:** Wash your hands thoroughly after touching animals or their feces. Wash your hands frequently, especially after using the toilet or before preparing food.

If you think you might be sick with cryptosporidosis, see a medical doctor.

To remain well hydrated, drink liquids, especially bottled water, often. Organisms such as cryptosporidium can be present in surface waters.

DEHYDRATION

Nutritionists recommend drinking eight large glasses of water every day just to maintain normal body functions. However, activities such as hiking and cross-country skiing will cause you to perspire and increase your need for water. To make sure you maintain adequate hydration in the mountains, try the suggestions below.

DEHYDRATION

• **DRINK LOTS OF WATER BEFORE ENGAGING IN A STRENUOUS SPORT SUCH AS MOUNTAIN HIKING:** Doing this ensures you will not be dehydrated before you start your trip. Since it is difficult to "over-hydrate" with normal kidney function, it is unlikely you will begin your trip with a surplus of hydration. One way to check whether your fluid levels are adequate is by monitoring your urine. It should be slightly yellow. If it is darker than this, you require more water to flush out the salts.

• **THIRST IS NOT A GOOD INDICATOR OF WHEN TO DRINK BECAUSE BY THE TIME YOUR MOUTH GETS DRY, YOU ARE ALREADY DEHYDRATED:** Make a point of drinking throughout the day before you get tired or thirsty. Your water requirements increase as your activity increases. As you heat up, your body cools itself by perspiring which causes you to lose water. How much water you need depends on factors such as your activity level, fitness, and the temperature and humidity of your environment.

• **GENERALLY, WATER OR UNSWEETENED JUICES ARE GOOD CHOICES:** Liquids that are too sweet slow the absorption of fluids into the bloodstream by osmosis. When the bloodstream is suddenly loaded with sugar, it stimulates an overproduction of insulin from the pancreas. This causes a condition called reactive hypoglycemia or low blood sugar.

• **DRINK MORE THAN YOU MIGHT IMAGINE YOU NEED WHEN IT IS COLD OUT:** Cold air is drier than warm air. In the winter, you use water and energy as your lungs and throat warm and moisten the cold air that you breathe in. And when

DEHYDRATION
(continued)

ELK

EXPOSURE

FLASH
FLOODS

you breathe out, you also lose moisture. That is why you can "see your breath" when it is cold. During cold temperatures, you lose water in other ways as well. For example, urine production increases in a process called cold dieresis.

• **AVOID DRINKING WATER THAT IS AT A TEMPERATURE NEAR FREEZING:** Your body expends energy when it warms it to body temperature. On the other hand, drinking warm water provides you with a slight amount of heat. Drink warm fluids rather than cold liquids during the winter. Eating snow also expends energy and takes heat away from you. If the snow is very cold, it can injure your throat or mouth lining. However, if you have no other liquids and are dehydrated, it is better to either eat snow or drink cold water than not drink anything at all. If you still have some water left in your water bottle, you can create more liquids by placing a bit of snow in it and shaking it or carrying it near your body until it melts. Or you can create water by melting snow. If you have some water, place it in the pot first, and then slowly add the snow. It melts more easily in this way.

• **AVOID INGESTING EXCESSIVE CAFFEINE, TOBACCO, AND ALCOHOL:** The caffeine in coffee may give you a kick-start but it is also a diuretic. By causing water loss, caffeine increases dehydration. Similar to caffeine, alcohol increases dehydration. And by dilating the blood vessels in your skin, it causes you to lose heat more quickly. Alcohol also cuts down on the liver's glucose production. Tobacco acts as a vasoconstrictor and increases your risk of frostbite.

ELK
See WAPITI

EXPOSURE
See HYPOTHERMIA

FLASH FLOODS
Unlike floods, which build slowly, flash floods occur quickly and with little warning. A flash flood can reach its peak in a few hours or even a few minutes. The force of the swiftly moving water carves out everything in its path including obstructions such as boulders, trees, and bridges. Some experts estimate it takes only 6 inches / 15 centimeters of swiftly moving water to knock a person over. In the United States, flash floodsare the number one weather-related killer. Flash floods can also trigger dangerous mudslides (see MUDSLIDES).

• **FLASH FLOOD HAZARDOUS AREAS:** Flash floods are caused in part by excessive rainfall, or by thunderstorms that move repeatedly over an area. The occurrence of a flash flood depends on factors such as the intensity and the duration of the rainfall as well as the proximity to natural floodplains and low-lying terrain. In addition to places near water and low-lying areas, canyons are also hazardous during a flash flood. Canyons have been slowly carved out over millions of years by the force of moving water. When a thunderstorm occurs, the rain naturally flows down from the land above and into the canyon below. The water accumulates in the bottom of the canyon and is naturally funneled along its path. If people are inside the canyon, they can become trapped by quickly rising water. Areas downstream of natural or human-constructed dams are also hazardous places to be during flash floods. Excessive rainfall and melting snow increases the load on the dam. If it fails, the entire contents of the reservoir are released at once and quickly surge downstream, sweeping away everything in its path. Natural obstructions can also cause flooding upstream.

• **AVOIDING AND MANAGING IN FLASH FLOOD CONDITIONS:** First, be alert to the possibility of flash flood conditions by watching the weather, listening to a battery-operated radio, and reading information posted in campgrounds. If conditions are ripe for flash floods, avoid hazardous mountain areas such as places near watercourses, flood plains, low-lying areas, canyons, and areas downstream of dams. Do not camp on low ground beside riverbeds or along smaller canyon streams if flood conditions are threatening. Flash floods can occur at night so it is especially important to be vigilant at this time. Plan an evacuation route and make sure all members of your party are aware of it. If you are caught in a flash flood in the mountains, immediately climb to higher ground and stay there until floodwaters recede. Do not attempt to walk through floodwaters, as the water may be deeper than it appears and the bed underneath may not be stable. If you are in a vehicle, do not attempt to drive through a flooded area. Turn around and drive to a safer area. If the vehicle stalls, or the floodwaters rise up around it, abandon the vehicle and move to higher ground.

FLASH
FLOODS
(continued)

FOREST FIRES

FROSTBITE

FOREST FIRES
See WILDFIRES

FROSTBITE
Frostbite is a cold injury. It is produced when tissues of the body freeze. In the early stages, this often involves exposed parts such as the face and ears. The hands and feet are also susceptible to frostbite because the body conserves heat by constricting blood vessels in the extremities. As the body cools, circulation slows and extremities and exposed tissue begin to freeze. Small ice crystals start to form within the cells. As the ice crystals grow, they expand, which physically damages the cells. Since the crystals take up water from the cells in this process, dehydration occurs. The chemical balance is also disturbed. In the early stages of frostbite, only small patches of exposed skin are affected. However, as frostbite progresses, deeper areas of tissue are involved. Deep frostbite can result in the loss of tissue or even a body part.

For frostbite to occur, the temperature must be below freezing. The skin itself must cool to a temperature between 22F to 24F (-5.5C to -4.4C). Other factors leading to frostbite include the tissue's length of contact with the cold. Tissue damage increases with the amount of time it remains frozen. The type of exposure is also a factor. For example, if the skin contacts cold metal, it can freeze very quickly. Since smoking cause the blood vessels in the skin to constrict, it can make cold injuries such as frostbite worse.

PREVENTING FROSTBITE
See Hypothermia Prevention since most of these principles apply to frostbite.

• PROTECT THE TRUNK OF THE BODY BY WEARING APPROPRIATE CLOTHING.

• PROTECT THE EXPOSED PARTS OF THE BODY SUCH AS FINGERS AND FACE BY WEARING MITTENS AND A SCARF OR FACEMASK.

• WEAR LOOSE CLOTHING SINCE TIGHTLY FITTING GARMENTS CONSTRICT CIRCULATION. MAKE SURE BOOTS ARE NOT LACED UP TOO TIGHTLY.

- AVOID WEARING AN EXTRA PAIR OF SOCKS IF THIS CONSTRICTS CIRCULATION.

- EXERCISE THE FINGERS AND TOES TO MAINTAIN CIRCULATION.

- CHECK THE CONDITION OF YOUR FRIENDS' FACE AND EARS FOR THE PRESENCE OF FROSTBITE. IF FROSTBITE IS DEVELOPING, TREAT IT IMMEDIATELY.

- AVOID SMOKING IF FROSTBITE IS A CONCERN.

FROSTBITE
(continued)

TREATING FROSTBITE

It is important to recognize frostbite in the early stages and treat it before it gets worse. Treat superficial frostbite by warming the area, and then protecting it from freezing again. However, do not treat deep frostbite by warming. Thawing a frostbitten part and then refreezing it causes the greatest tissue damage. See Treating Frostbite chart below.

Treating Frostbite

SUPERFICIAL FROSTBITE	SIGNS AND SYMPTOMS	TREATMENT (backcountry)
	Sensations of pain early on, which disappear as the tissues freeze. The tissue can appear white in color and feel waxy. When pressed, the freezing tissue will indent.	• Treat superficial frostbite immediately. • Warm the frostbitten tissue so it does not become further frostbitten. • Do this by placing the frostbitten tissue next to a warm body part such as an armpit. • Do not rub the tissue or rub snow on it. • Do not let the thawed tissue freeze.
DEEP FROSTBITE	SIGNS AND SYMPTOMS	TREATMENT (backcountry)
	As the tissue continues to freeze, it becomes number. Eventually, all sensation in the frozen area is lost. The victim cannot move the affected joint. The tissue feels quite hard. When pressed, the skin will not indent.	• Do not thaw frostbitten tissue and then allow it to refreeze. Instead, keep the frozen part frozen. • Do not rub it. • Do not allow the victim to bear weight on the frostbitten tissue. Carry out someone with frostbitten feet. • Provide the victim with fluids. • Evacuate the victim and seek medical attention.

Left: It is important to recognize frostbite in the early stages and treat it before it gets worse.

GIARDIASIS

GIARDIASIS

Giardia lamblia, a single-celled parasite, is found worldwide. Referred to as *Giardia intestinalis* in some regions, the parasite produces giardiasis, the most frequent cause of non-bacterial diarrhea in North America. People can carry the disease without displaying any symptoms.

According to experts, giardia is widespread in the backcountry. Because of increased backcountry use, more cases of giardia are being reported. Giardia is of particular concern in areas with cold surface waters such as the Pacific Northwest and the Rocky Mountains. There tends to be higher concentrations of giardia cysts in the spring and fall.

GIARDIA

Giradia has two forms, both of which are larger than bacteria. The pear-shaped trophozoite is non-infectious while the cyst is infectious. The trophozoite attaches to a person's upper small intestine using a disc-shaped suction pad. Here, it feeds and reproduces by binary fission, which enables it to increase its numbers rapidly. Once it releases its hold, it floats through the intestine using its whip-like flagella and changes into its second form, a cyst. Although the trophozoite may only survive for a few hours outside a person's body, the cyst, about 1/100 of millimeter in length, is hardier. As the survival form of the parasite, the cyst is resistant to adverse conditions, although it favors a cool moist environment.

Unlike the trophozoite, it can infect both people and animals. The giardia cyst is passed in the feces of infected persons or animals. If people drink water contaminated by feces, they swallow the cysts. Their stomach acids and digestive enzymes free the trophozoites, and they begin to reproduce.

GIARDIASIS SYMPTOMS

Relating to the gastrointestinal tract, giardiasis can result in acute diarrhea, cramps, nausea, bloating, flatulence, loss of weight, poor appetite, and tiredness. Symptoms vary throughout the course of the disease, and different individuals infected with the same strain can show different symptoms.

While some can have mild diarrhea or no symptoms, others may have chronic diarrhea for weeks and suffer from significant weight loss. Although giardiasis generally lasts for about one to two weeks, chronic infections can last for a few months or even years.

Chronic cases of symptomatic giardiasis occur in adults more often than children and are associated with malabsorption of nutrients and severe weight loss. Increased flatulence and cramps, loose stools, fatigue, and depression mark this phase. Lactose intolerance occurs in about 40% of those infected. After consuming milk products, discomfort increases.

SOURCES OF GIARDIA

Although water from a mountain stream often looks sparkling clear, it may be swarming with bacteria and other micro-organisms. Rain can wash giardia-contaminated human waste from outhouses, cabin toilets, and backcountry sites into water sources. In addition, pet dogs can be infected and then become a source of infection for people.

Beavers and muskrats defecate in or near the water and so play a role in giardia transmission. Beavers are easily infected with giardia from people. The giardia reproduces in the beaver, and then the animals return millions of cysts into the water. Giardia is sometimes called "beaver fever" because of the amplifying role that beavers play in disease transmission but studies show human waste can be just as significant. Most human giardia infections come from other humans and humans infect beaver with giardia.

In the United States, a study showed that beaver living in remote backcountry areas had a low rate of giardia infection. But those living downstream of national forest campgrounds had a higher rate of giardia. Other mammals such as bear, squirrel, and skunk have also been found to have giardia.

Unlike surface water, water from deep wells generally does not contain giardia because it is filtered as the water percolates downward through the ground. Giardia can also occur in urban settings or countries where water has not been adequately filtered. Although giardia is transmitted most frequently through contaminated water, it can be spread through contaminated food or infected food handlers.

PREVENTING GIARDIASIS

Since giardia is primarily transmitted through human or animal fecal contamination of water or food, there are several measures you can take to prevent getting it.

• **WHEN IN THE BACKCOUNTRY, DO NOT CONTAMINATE A WATER SOURCE, GROUNDWATER, OR SURFACE WATER WITH WASTE:** This might result in contaminated waste washing into the water source transmitting giardia to people and other animals.

• **TAKE SAFE DRINKING WATER WITH YOU:** Since you cannot tell if water from a source such as a backcountry stream is safe to drink by its appearance, drink the water you carry instead of water from a stream.

• **IF YOU CANNOT CARRY AN ADEQUATE WATER SUPPLY, PURIFY IT BY BOILING, CHEMICAL DISINFECTANTS, OR FILTERS:** Find the clearest water available to purify such as clean water containing aquatic life. If the water has no vegetation or large amounts of green algae, it is probably bad water. If the water appears cloudy, use a cloth to strain it before applying the chemical disinfectant. This gets rid of some of the sediment (and pathogens attached to it). Or, let the water settle before treating it. Since the amount of iodine and the disinfecting time varies, follow the recommendations provided by the manufacturer. The *St. John's Ambulance Guide* cautiously recommends a minimum contact time of eight hours to be sure of killing giardia.

—**BOILING:** Boiling water vigorously for about two or three minutes at sea level will kill all pathogens including viruses and protozoans such as giardia. It will also make the water taste flat. However, you will need to boil the water longer at higher elevations. Boil water for about four minutes at 5,000 feet / 1,500 meters. Increase the boiling time by five minutes each time you gain another 5,000 feet / 1,500 meters. Although boiling requires a stove and fuel as well as time, it is an uncomplicated way to purify water.

—**IODINE:** When used properly, iodine kills most pathogens as well as viruses. It is lightweight, easy to carry and inexpensive. However, it affects the taste of the water, and its effectiveness varies depending on the purity of the water, its temperature and pH. The dirtier the water, the more iodine you will require. You need to judge how much iodine is needed while ensuring you do not ingest too much of the chemical. In addition, replace iodine tablets each year because its potency is limited. Caution: If taken for extended periods of time (longer than about two weeks) or in large quantities, iodine can effect a person adversely. If you have a health problem affected by iodine such as a thyroid condition, or if you are pregnant,

GIARDIASIS
(continued)

Giardia: Any of various flagellated, usually non-pathogenic protozoa of the genus Giardia that may be parasitic in the intestines of vertebrates including human beings and most domestic animals.

—After Alfred Mathieu Giard, 1846-1908, French zoologist.

The Scoop on Poop:

Dixon Thompson

An interview with Dixon Thompson, a mountaineer, environmental scientist, and expert in backcountry waste management issues.

What is meant by "cumulative impacts?"

DT: Well, no one hiker taking one dump in the backcountry is in itself a significant impact. However, when there are increasing numbers of people doing so, it produces a cumulative impact. This is understood when it comes to litter. One person throwing a piece of paper on the trail once is not a problem. But it is a problem if many people do it all the time.

Does voluntary action presuppose an attitude change on the part of backcountry users?

DT: It comes down to the kind of philosophy that was behind the ethical behavior in the backcountry conference that I organized for the Alpine Club of Canada (ACC) [ACC Symposium on Water, Energy and Waste Management in Alpine Shelters, October 1991] some years ago. That is, we have to take steps to protect the quality of the environment that attracted us to the mountains in the first place. And that is going to mean that as more and more people go there, more and more stringent actions have to be taken to ensure that the increasing number of people does not degrade the environment.

For beginning hikers, outhouses are still the way to go?

DT: For the most part, beginners are out on trails where there are outhouses provided. And that means taking the attitude that "let's everybody go to the bathroom before we start off, and let's take advantage of the facilities now rather than waiting until you are way down the trail and you say, "Oh gee . . . nature calls." But

beginners can still get into some areas where "pack it out" will be the normal practice. For example, climbers in Cougar Canyon near Banff National Park, Alberta, are advised to use the outhouse there or pack it out because there is just too many people and too little soil to find a suitable area to bury it. And so the same advice would apply to hikers visiting the canyon.

When is burying waste an acceptable means of disposal?

DT: Soil bacteria can handle quite a bit of human waste, and so burying waste is the way we should go—until user density overwhelms the soil's capacity to handle it or where low temperature conditions prevent that from occurring. And until you are digging catholes in other catholes, and it is becoming a visual problem. Hikers do not like to see shit or toilet paper in the backcountry and when it becomes really bad, it becomes an odor problem. You should also note that in almost all cases, urine is sterile. Its main contribution to the environment is the addition of nutrients. There is a very slow growth rate in eutrophic waters, which is due to the cold temperature of the water and the lack of nutrients. And so when you add nutrients one of those constraints is removed and that may contribute to eutrophication. But it is less of a visual, less of an aesthetic problem.

Managing Human Waste in the Backcountry

What is involved in packing waste out?

DT: I would recommend using a plastic container with a snap-on lid. Line it with a plastic bag. Put some kitty litter or some zeolite (a natural mineral) between the plastic bag and the plastic container. It is highly absorbent in terms of odor and moisture, and so if some spillage occurs, you do not have it leaking. And then most people carry duct tape in their backcountry repair kit. Take a strip of duct tape and seal the container. It means you have an extra volume in your pack, but that is the price we have to pay for protecting the environment we went to see in the first place.

On longer journeys—say a 10-day backpacking trip—that could really add up.

DT: Well, remember that you are not going to be packing out urine if you can learn to control yourself. You are only going to be packing out the feces. Presumably there is some kind of balance between the food you pack in to eat, and the feces you produce as a result of consuming the food. So...you do the arithmetic.

Is it acceptable to use other methods such as smearing it on a rock to speed drying or throwing it into a crevasse?

DT: Well, let's start with the smearing. I do not know of any place where that would be acceptable. Presumably where it is dry enough and hot enough that it would dry effectively in the sun-

light and the ultraviolet radiation in the sunlight would sterilize it. But who would want to see shit smeared on rocks until the next windstorm or rainstorm? As far as throwing it into a crevasse—using a green garbage bag and disposing of the garbage bag in a crevasse has been the accepted practice in some areas. However, at the rate of retreat of our glaciers, I do wonder when we are going to start seeing some of those garbage bags . . . but maybe the pressure of the moving ice will take care of it.

Is burying it under snow acceptable?

DT: Burying it under snow? I don't think so. That is what to led to a problem with human waste on some of the routes on Mount McKinley for example. The areas around some of the popular campsites became so contaminated with feces, that when you were melting snow to produce water for cooking and drinking, you discovered that someone had taken a dump in it. So let's forget about that one.

What about paper? Burn it, bury it, or pack it out?

DT: Some backcountry areas require you to dig a cathole to bury the feces but to carry the paper out. I suppose that is on the basis that the feces will incorporate itself into the soil faster than the paper. If the density of use were not high enough to warrant packing the paper out, probably burying it would be an option. Let's put it this way: where park regu-

lations advise you to burn your paper, do so; where regulations advise you to pack out the paper, do so. I do not think there is any point in women digging a cathole to pee but if you use paper then that might be an instance where you would want to burn it or pack it out instead of leaving it around.

Do you think people will warm up to the idea of packing it out in the future?

DT: Well, when I first raised this with the Alpine Club of Canada more than 10 years ago, the response was very negative. People were just not prepared to even think about putting shit into their packs. And at the time, we were not yet facing a high enough density of use that it was a problem. We were still able to rely on outhouses at the alpine club huts and that sort of thing. So the reluctance to think about it—"I'm not going to put shit in my pack"—was understandable. But there has been considerable change since that time. Let's put it this way: years ago people went out into the wilderness and chopped down trees and built shelters. And they kept chopping down trees and building shelters. And they chopped down trees and put the pine boughs in their bedding. And now, doing that is an absolute "no-no." And so, yes, in time I expect that "packing it out" will just become part of the accepted way that people do things.

G

GIARDIASIS
(continued)

avoid using iodine. Keep iodine in a sealed container since it can oxidize materials such as metal. Avoid leaving it unsealed in a tent or other closed space, since it may produce poisonous levels of toxic fumes. After you add the disinfectant, shake the water in a sealed container to thoroughly mix the disinfectant. Disinfectants work more efficiently in warm water. If you are purifying water from a glacial stream, leave the disinfectant in the water for a longer period of time. If the water is noticeably dirty, it also takes longer to disinfect it. Use a higher concentration of disinfectant if the water is very cold or dirty. A higher concentration increases the probability of killing the giardia cysts.

—**FILTERS:** Instead of attempting to destroy pathogens by either boiling or chemical disinfectants, you can also use a portable filter to remove them from the water. As you pump water through the filter, it allows water to pass through but stops micro-organisms. Unlike iodine, filters can improve the taste of the water. There are a number of filters available commercially and they vary in expense and effectiveness. A filter with a screen of at least 0.2 microns (a micron is equal to one millionth of a meter) will remove most pathogens and bacteria. A screen of 1.0 micron is required for giardia since it is a larger micro-organism. When selecting a filter, consider factors such as durability. For example, a well-designed filter will stop unfiltered water from leaking into filtered water. A removable filter enables you to clean or replace it easily. A high-quality filter will provide a high output.

—**IODINE AND FILTRATION:** Since viruses are small in size, filters are not always effective at removing them. If you require protection against viruses, disinfect water with iodine. If done properly, this method should remove all pathogens including viruses. However, the iodine will affect the taste of the water. In addition, doing both of these things is more time consuming than using the other methods. Note that in North America viruses are not usually of concern in the backcountry.

—**PURIFIERS:** Purifiers are filters with built in iodination. They should remove all pathogens including viruses. Because both filtering and iodination occur within one unit, purifiers are easier to use than performing both of these tasks separately. In addition, some purifiers can limit the taste and exposure to iodine. Purifiers are generally more expensive than filters. For backcountry users, filters are generally the most effective way of preventing giardiasis. Chemical disinfectants, such as iodine, are more problematic because of all of the factors involved in their effectiveness.

TREATING GIARDIASIS

Giardiasis is generally medically diagnosed through personal history and stool examination. Tests are available for human feces as well as for rats, dogs, cattle, and sheep. In the test, cysts or trophozoites are detected in stained or unstained fecal smears using a microscope.

The success rate of the examination is estimated at about 50-70%. It requires a trained technician and a number of specimens can be required. Since the parasite is not always easily detected in the stool, some people require a biopsy of the stomach or small bowel. In addition, blood samples can be used to look for antibody type. Drug therapy is available to treat giardiasis.

"The icefall was crisscrossed with crevasses and tottering seracs. From afar it brought to mind a bad train wreck, as if scores of ghostly white boxcars had derailed at the lip of the ice cap and tumbled down the slope willy-nilly."

—*Jon Krakauer*

Proper equipment and training are essential to safely travel on glacier terrain.

GLACIERS

GLACIERS

Glaciers are found in high latitudes or in high mountain ranges. Snow falling in the high mountains collects especially during the winter, because it melts more slowly than it falls. Over time, the snow on the bottom layers is pressed together and transformed into ice. The compressed layers eventually form a glacier, a year-round ice mass. When a glacier attains a depth of about 100 feet / 30 meters, it slowly migrates from the high alpine toward the valley below. The glacier continues to creep forward as long as an abundance of snow continues to fall.

Because of the tremendous weight of the ice, layers on the bottom of the glacier are quite dense. However, as the ice creeps downward, the upper layers begin to crack under the stress. These cracks are called crevasses. When the glacier flows rapidly over a very steep slope, it creates a profusion of crevasses called an icefall. The crevasses that make up the icefall move as the glacier advances. This creates an unstable mass of cracks and ice debris. Large towers of ice, called seracs, are created as ice breaks away from the glacier. Since seracs can collapse unexpectedly as the glacier advances, being in their vicinity is extremely hazardous. When mountaineers are forced to travel under a serac, they move as quickly as possible and do not stop until they are out of danger.

Crevasses are created as the glacier creeps around corners or as it flows over obstructions underlying the ice. They can also be produced because the ice moves at different rates. For example, the center of the glacier may advance more quickly than the edges. These cracks, which can attain a depth of some 250 feet / 76 meters, are one of the principal hazards of glacier travel. Since crevasses can be completely or partially filled with snow, they can be difficult to identify. Snow-cover can also produce a false sense of security. Blowing or falling snow makes detection difficult. Once in a crevasse, it may be virtually impossible to get out without the proper equipment. The result can be physical injury, hypothermia or death. If you want to explore a glacier, go with a professionally guided group, or first get instruction in glacier travel and crevasse rescue.

When a layer of snow forms over a crevasse, a snowbridge is formed. Depend-

"The glaciers are the pass-makers, and it is by them that the courses of all mountaineers are predestined."

—John Muir

ing on the strength of the bridge, people can cross the crevasse safely or they can fall in if the snowbridge gives way. The strength of the snowbridge weakens by the movement of the glacier and by changing weather.

As it advances, the glacier accumulates rocky debris. It falls upon the glacier from the headwall. It is deposited on the glacier as the glacier scrapes the sides of the valley. It is also brought into the glacier from its rocky bed. The tumbled-up debris eventually creates a glacial feature called a moraine.

There are several kinds of moraine. A lateral moraine is created from deposits of debris along the sides of the glacier. Lateral moraines can form on the ice itself or along its sides. A medial moraine is created when lateral moraines from two nearby valleys come together. The medial moraine forms in the middle of the glacier that is created by the merging of the two valley glaciers. A terminal moraine—created at the lower end of the glacier—is composed primarily of the rocky material pushed along by the glacier as it moves along the valley.

Glacial moraines are often very hard and very steep. As well as a jumble of rocky debris, they can contain a mix of sand and silt that make them unsteady. Some glacial moraines contain ice that makes the surface slippery. In the heat of the sun, the ice can melt and turn the surrounding moraine into a mire of mud-covered rock. Large boulders within the moraine can break loose from the melting debris and cause hazards from rockfall.

When the glacier reaches a lower altitude where more snow melts than falls, it begins to thaw and forms meltwater channels. The channels may run along the surface of the glacier, flow into crevasses, or disappear into chutes called mill-wells. The water runs below or within the ice and eventually emerges at the end of the glacier. Falling into a millwell is extremely hazardous since the person may become jammed underneath the glacier and be very difficult to extract.

With the heat of the sun, small meltwater channels surge into torrents that are difficult to cross. The meltwater streams or rivers forming at the toe of the glacier contain deposits of silt or rock flour, a white-colored substance composed of small pieces of rock ground by glacial movement. Avoid crossing a glacial steam heavy with silt since it can act like quicksand and trap unwary travelers in the muck. It is advisable to avoid drinking water from glacial streams since the silt may cause stomach upset. However, if that is your only option, allow the silt to settle before drinking.

The flow of water on glaciers slows during the cool mountain nights. Crossing can be much easier early in the morning. But do not forget that it will be trickier if you must return by the same route later in the day.

TIPS FOR SAFE GLACIER TRAVEL

Glaciers have large cracks called crevasses. If a person falls into a crevasse and cannot get out, he or she will probably quickly die of hypothermia and other injuries. For this reason and other objective hazards, respect glaciers.

- **BEFORE VENTURING UPON A GLACIER:** Take a course in glacier travel. Practise crevasse rescue techniques until they become second nature.

- **LEARN BASIC NAVIGATION SKILLS:** Become proficient at using map and compass since whiteouts are common.

- **LEARN HOW TO BUILD BASIC SHELTERS:** The weather could change quickly and obscure hazards such as icefalls, crevasses, and cliffs. The most prudent choice might be to stay put until the weather clears.

- **LEARN HOW TO PROVIDE FIRST AID FOR COLD INJURIES SUCH AS HYPOTHERMIA AND FROSTBITE:** Because of their elevation, glaciers are colder than surrounding lowlands.

"Before I could plot a logical course through the icefall, the wind came up, and snow began to slant hard out of the clouds, stinging my face and reducing visibility to almost nothing."

—Jon Krakauer

Tips for Navigating in Whiteouts

These mountaineers are using a rope to increase their safety while traveling in a whiteout.

When a whiteout occurs on a snowfield or glacier, it reduces visibility dramatically. Everything literally turns white. It becomes difficult to distinguish terrain features or even tell where a drift of snow ends and the horizon begins. In severe whiteouts, it may be impossible to see even a few feet. This poses serious problems in keeping on route. Many people have become disoriented or lost due to whiteout conditions. Poor visibility can also cause mountain travelers to wander into steep terrain such as cliff bands or difficult terrain such as canyons. Getting off the main trail, skiers may become bogged down in deep snow.

Having a map and compass and knowing how to use them correctly helps you keep on route during whiteouts. So does a global positioning system (GPS). However, if you are not proficient in these navigation techniques, there are still some practical things you can do to help keep on course.

• **Keep an eye on the weather throughout your trip.** If it looks like bad weather is coming in, which may restrict visibility, discontinue your trip. Do not wait until visibility is so poor that you cannot see your tracks. Instead, turn around and follow your trail or ski tracks back to your starting point while you can still see.

• **If you do get stuck in a whiteout and do not have good navigation skills, do not wander around.** This can result in your becoming lost or getting into difficult terrain. Instead, sit down and wait. Put on extra clothing to keep yourself warm. Although some whiteouts can last for extended periods of time, others may clear quite quickly. Once you can again see your route, turn around. Continue only if the weather has cleared or if you are confident you can stay on route.

• **Watch for any breaks in the weather while you are waiting.** A momentary clearing might reveal a peak or other landmark that you can identify.

• **If you are traveling in a whiteout and cannot tell whether the terrain is rising or falling, throw a rock or snowball on the ground ahead of you.** You will be able to see whether it is going up or down, and this can help you decide whether to proceed in a certain direction.

• **If you decide to go either ahead or retrace your steps in poor visibility, keep to your trail.** It is a definite feature in an otherwise featureless landscape and will help prevent you from becoming lost or further lost.

• **Travel cautiously.** If you cannot see where you are going, proceed carefully. Otherwise it is possible you can end up someplace that you do not want to be such as at the edge of a cliff.

HANTAVIRUS

HANTAVIRUS PULMONARY SYNDROME (HPS)

Hantavirus Pulmonary Syndrome was first identified after an outbreak of fatal respiratory disease occurred in the southwestern United States in 1993. The disease is characterized by symptoms such as fever, aching muscles and headache. As it progresses, it effects the lung and causes death about half the time.

Rodents such as deermice and cotton rats are host to hantaviruses, and HPS virus is widespread wherever deermice occur. In the United States, deermice, which live in a variety of rural habitats, are considered to be the primary host of the hantavirus that is of greatest medical concern. However, other mammals such as pinon mice, western chipmunks, and brush mice may carry different forms of hantavirus. Researchers believe specific hantaviruses favor specific rodent hosts.

Once infected, the rodent hosts do not become ill; however they release the virus in their urine, feces and saliva. You can pick up the virus in a number of ways: By contacting or inhaling material contaminated with the urine or feces of infected rodents or by getting bitten by an infected rodent. Transmission time is short: A few minutes of exposure is all it may take. Although it is possible to pick up the virus from contaminated food or water, research suggests the virus has not been transmitted from person to person or from insects such as ticks and mosquitoes.

Scientists are unsure how long hantaviruses may live once in the environment but weak disinfectants such as dilute hydrochloride solutions, ethyl alcohol and detergents will kill them.

TIPS FOR AVOIDING HPS

The best way to avoid HPS is to avoid the rodents that carry it. If you are in the backcountry, following these rules can minimize your risk.

• **HIKERS AND BACKPACKERS:** Since you can get HPS by inhaling the dust of contaminated urine or feces, do not disturb any places where rodents such as deermice, pack rats, or other small mammals nest. This includes dens, burrows, brush, woodpiles or other places small animals call home. Follow the same rules you use for keeping your campsite free of bears and other animals. Keep food in sealed containers. Dispose of garbage in bins or store well away from your campsite and sleeping areas. Avoid leaving anything lying around that might attract small rodents and other mammals, particularly at night.

When you choose your campsite, look around and make sure you are not camping on or near dens, burrows, brush, or woodpiles. Instead of sleeping on the ground out in the open, sleep in a tent with a secure floor.

Trappers, hunters, and hikers have used backcountry shelters over the years without contracting HPS. On the other hand, small mammals burrow under cabins and backcountry huts leaving behind contaminated feces or urine, and it is possible that you could get HPS in this manner.

Look around for signs of rodent use: Litter, small heaps of trash or little piles of wood, mouse droppings, and food that has been gnawed. If you are staying in a cabin and are concerned about rodent use, clean the area using disinfectant and plastic gloves if they are available. If there are signs of severe rodent use, contact a local health official for information about how to safeguard yourself while decontaminating the shelter.

Avoiding rodents helps avoid the hantaviruses they might carry.

HANTAVIRUS
(continued)

• **RURAL DWELLERS:** While hikers and campers can be at risk of contracting HPS by being in the outdoors, people who live in rural areas or stay in cabins can also be at risk. If you are staying in a rural cabin or shelter for an extended period of time, consider these additional steps to minimize the risk of getting the disease.

Make sure your cabin is tightly closed and that small mammals cannot get into it. Put screens around your windows and doors. Close off any openings that are one quarter of an inch in size or greater.

Follow many of the same procedures for keeping a clean campsite. Make sure you store your food and garbage securely; avoid providing rodents with a food source. Store your outdoor garbage bins about a foot off of the ground. Get rid of things in your yard such as piles of brush, woodpiles, or tires that rodents might nest in. Keep your wood about 100 feet / 30 meters away from your house and at least one foot / 30 centimeters off the ground.

Since food for your pets may also become food for rodents, either feed your pet inside the house or place your pet food 1 foot / .3 meters off the ground.

If you are concerned about rodents in and around your house, talk to your local health authority about decontamination. It's important to be careful since you may infect yourself while cleaning your cabin.

• **WORKERS IN THE OUTDOORS:** If you regularly work outdoors in areas where rodents may be infected, you might want to take some additional steps to minimize your risk. Find out which rodents inhabit the area you are working in. Familiarize yourself with their habitats. In this way, you can take extra steps to avoid them.

If you experience symptoms indicative of HPS within four to five days of possible exposure, seek medical advice. If you might be in contact with infected rodents, get information from your local health authority on protective clothing. This could include rubber gloves, goggles, and a respirator or filter that prevents you from breathing contaminated dust.

HEAT STRESS

HEAT STRESS

The normal temperature of your body is 96.6°F / 37°C. If your temperature rises to 100°F / 38°C, you do not feel well. If your temperature rises to 104°F / 40°C, you become very ill. To maintain a normal core temperature, the cooling system of your body constantly monitors and regulates your internal temperature. As temperatures fluctuate, blood flows back and forth from your internal organs to your limbs. When you are under heat stress, the blood vessels open up increasing the flow of blood to the skin up to a hundred times. When your body cannot maintain a normal temperature, heat stress results.

Heat stress is caused by both external and internal mechanisms. External factors include high temperatures and humidity, while internal factors include inadequate fluid intake, overexertion, constitutional factors and sunburn. In the mountains, factors such as high temperatures, sunshine, high humidity, strenuous activity and dehydration can contribute to heat stress. Heat stress can occur at any time of the year. The two major problems associated with heat stress are heat exhaustion and heat stroke.

- **HEAT EXHAUSTION:** Heat exhaustion results from a significant increase in the core temperature of the body. It causes symptoms such as cramps, nausea, weakness, headache and disorientation. If someone suffers from heat exhaustion and does not continually improve after treatment, heat stroke may result.

- **HEAT STROKE:** Heat stroke, a life-threatening condition, is the most serious heat-related illness. It results from a number of factors such as prolonged exposure to high temperatures, strenuous exercise in high humidity and heat, inefficient sweat glands or a dysfunctional hypothalamus gland. When this occurs, the metabolism of the body no longer functions normally.

Since an above-normal body temperature affects a person both mentally and physically, someone suffering from heat stroke can become irrational, confused and uncoordinated. Nausea, vomiting, shortness of breath, a rapid pulse, and convulsions can occur. They can become unconscious and eventually die.

PREVENTING HEAT STRESS

By maintaining your fluid levels and electrolyte balance and by regulating your exposure to heat, you can prevent many heat-related problems. If you have any conditions that influence the ability of your body to regulate heat, seek advice from your doctor. These include fluid retention, fluid-restricted diets, epilepsy, certain medications, and heart, kidney or liver disease.

- **MAINTAIN ADEQUATE FLUID LEVELS:** Although you can function without food for a number of days, you cannot survive for very long without water. You need to replace the water you lose every day as a result of the normal functioning of your cooling and digestive systems as well as your excretory functions. With strenuous exercise such as mountain biking or hiking, the amount of water you require rises dramatically.

- **DRINK ADEQUATE AMOUNTS OF WATER:** Make sure you are well hydrated before you start your activity, whether it is winter or summer. Continue to drink regularly throughout the day, perhaps every half-hour, even if you are not thirsty. Bear in mind you may not feel thirsty until you have lost almost a quart / liter of water. You could also try some of the commercial athletic drinks designed to replace electrolytes. Eat light, cool meals instead of hot, heavy ones.

• **LIMIT ALCOHOL, CAFFEINE AND TEA:** Since alcohol contributes to dehydration, avoid alcohol under conditions which might produce heat-related illness. Alcohol also influences your judgment, which causes you to become less aware of impending heat exhaustion.

• **WATCH THE LEVEL OF SALT IN YOUR DIET:** Most people get enough salt from their regular diet, so taking extra salt is usually not necessary. If you ingest too much salt, you will have to drink more fluids to eliminate it from your system.

HEAT STRESS
(continued)

The kidneys only pass urine when it contains a certain concentration of salt (electrolytes). If there is too much salt in your system, water will be extracted from your blood to dilute the concentration of salt. Experts say you should only take salt tablets if prescribed by your physician. If you feel you need more salt, consider taking some light salted foods such as nuts or pretzels along with you. Munch on them throughout the day. However, if you do eat salted foods, make sure you drink lots of water.

• **WEAR LIGHT CLOTHING:** Light-colored clothing helps reflect heat and sunlight. Thus light colors such as beige are a better choice on a hot day than dark colors such as black. Make sure your clothing is loose fitting and allows heat to escape.

Some people like to wear a cotton T-shirt on hot summer days. When they perspire, the T-shirt gets wet and the moisture helps keep them cool. Wear a wide-brimmed hat that covers your head and neck to protect yourself from the sun or use an umbrella. Some hikers travel with an umbrella rain or shine. The umbrella keeps them dry if it rains and keeps them cool if it is hot and sunny.

• **REGULATE YOUR EXPOSURE TO HEAT AND SUNSHINE:** Since heat produces physiological changes in the body, give your body time to get used to it. Doing this can moderate the effects of heat over the short term. In addition, going from one temperature extreme to another may be hazardous. For example, if it is hot outside and you jump into a glacial lake to cool off, the sudden cold can produce mental and physical stress. The elderly or the very young might experience hypothermia.

"We are on a steep learning curve when it comes to HPS."

—Margo Pybus

How the Body Regulates Its Core Temperature

Since it is important to maintain a stable temperature, the body has built-in mechanisms that recognize variations in temperature both in the core and in the periphery.

The hypothalamus, which is located in the brain, responds to changes in core blood temperature. As your environment and activity either cools or heats your body, control mechanisms come into play to either increase or decrease heat loss.

• **Perspiration:** When you become too hot, you perspire, which takes moisture from your body tissues to the surface of your skin. As it evaporates, it takes the latent heat of evaporation from your skin and cools you down.

• **Shivering:** When receptors in your brain and skin sense cold, you start to shiver. As blood pumps into your muscles, and they contract and expand, heat is produced through an increase in chemical reactions generating heat five times faster than your basal metabolic rate. However, producing heat from shivering only last a few hours because your muscle glucose will become depleted. How long you shiver depends on how many carbohydrates and how much oxygen and water is available.

• **Vasoconstriction:** When the flow of blood to your periphery, for example, your toes and hands, is decreased, heat loss is also decreased.

• **Vasodilatation:** When the flow of blood to the surface of your skin increases, heat loss also increases.

HEAT STRESS
(continued)

• **MODIFY YOUR ACTIVITIES TO REDUCE HEAT STRESS:** Exercise generates heat and so the harder you work, the hotter you get. In the mountains, energy expenditure is determined by a number of factors such as your pace, your load (both the weights of your body and your pack), and whether you are traveling uphill, downhill or over difficult terrain. Your conditioning also plays a part, since out-of-shape people generally work harder than the fit.

The more strenuous the activity, the more demand on your heart, and the more heat you generate. If you do exercise strenuously in the heat, take regular breaks even if you do not feel tired. This gives your body the chance to recuperate and cool off. If there is a cold stream nearby, stop and dangle your feet in it. Water is a good conductor and moving water removes heat about 25 times faster than cool air.

• **TAKE CARE OF CHILDREN AND ANIMALS:** Avoid placing children and animals in situations where heat stress could result.

TREATING HEAT-RELATED CONDITIONS

The general treatment for heat stress is to get the person out of the heat and help them cool down. Treat heat cramps and heat exhaustion immediately. If you do not, heat exhaustion could develop into heat stroke. CAUTION:

—**AVOID GIVING ANY STIMULANTS SUCH AS ALCOHOL OR CIGARETTES:** Alcohol causes further dehydration. Cigarettes shut down peripheral blood flow and reduces further heat loss.

—**AVOID PUTTING ICE DIRECTLY ON THE SKIN:** Placing ice or cold substances directly on the skin can result in too rapid cooling.

—**AVOID LEAVING THE PATIENT ALONE:** Watch vital signs such as breathing and heart rate. Ensure that their condition is improving.

• **CRAMPS AND HEAT EXHAUSTION**

—**MASSAGE CRAMPED MUSCLES:** One of the first signs the body is having difficulty dealing with the heat is sudden, painful; muscle contractions or spasms in your abdomen or legs called heat cramps. Heat cramps do not usually last longer than about 15 minutes. Have the person rest in a cool place. Gently massage the muscles, and make sure the person is well hydrated. They should be able to resume activity that day.

—**GET OUT OF THE HEAT:** Reduce exposure to the sun or heat in whatever way you can. Find a shady place or a cool area near an outcrop or other natural feature. If you cannot find a natural feature, make some kind of shelter using available resources.

—**STRETCH AND MASSAGE CRAMPED MUSCLES:** If the patient is suffering from heat cramps, gently stretch and massage the muscles. Since cramps are produced by a combination of vigorous exercise and inadequate fluid intake, encourage the patient to rest. This will give them a chance to restore their body temperature.

—**COOL THE PATIENT:** Cool the patient by applying damp compresses to the head, neck, groin, and armpits. Since these areas are close to major arteries, applying compresses there helps reduce the core temperature. If you do not have compresses, improvise with a T-shirt or other article of clothing. If that is not available, use cool water. Try fanning them. If their clothing is tight, loosen it so their clothing breathes and their body has a chance to cool down. Avoid cooling them down to the point that they get goosebumps or start to shiver.

HEAT STRESS
(continued)

—**PROVIDE SIPS OF FLUIDS IF THEY ARE CONSCIOUS:** In intervals of about 15 minutes, provide sips of water, juice or commercial preparations containing electrolytes to slowly replenish their fluid levels. If they become nauseous or vomit, stop. Flavored water may decrease nausea; adding salt to unflavored water may increase it. Replace electrolytes once the patient recovers. Replenish electrolytes by providing fluids or food containing salt. Make sure the patient maintains an adequate water intake.

—**MONITOR VITAL SIGNS:** Continue to monitor their breathing and consciousness. Make sure their body temperature normalizes. Casualties should not resume activity until they are completely recovered. If possible, have them rest for the remainder of the day. Continue to watch them carefully for any signs of heat stress such as changes in consciousness, refusing to drink water or vomiting. Vomiting leads to further dehydration.

• HEAT STROKE

Since heat stroke is life threatening, give the casualty immediate attention. Try to reduce their high internal (core) temperature. (Note: It may be difficult for someone who is not trained in first aid to determine whether or not to give fluids. **CAUTION:**

—**AVOID GIVING THE CASUALTY ANY FLUIDS:** Since they are dehydrated and have little circulation, fluids will not be absorbed. Giving fluids to a person suffering from heat stroke could cause them to vomit and inhale it. However, if you avoid giving fluids, you must be very certain you are dealing with a person who is suffering from heat stroke. If the person is suffering from heat exhaustion instead of heat stroke, withholding fluids could lead to stroke and possibly death.

—**AVOID PROVIDING AN OVER-THE-COUNTER MEDICATION:** Since the circulation of the casualty is decreased, the medication may not be absorbed. It could sit in the stomach and cause local damage such as an ulcer or vomiting.

—**AVOID GIVING ANY STIMULANTS SUCH AS ALCOHOL OR CIGARETTES:** Alcohol causes dehydration while cigarettes shut down peripheral blood flow and puts stress on the body core.

—**AVOID PUTTING ICE DIRECTLY ON THE SKIN AS THIS MAY RESULT IN TOO RAPID COOLING:** If the person cools down too quickly, it could stress the system and result in hypothermia.

—**AVOID LEAVING THE CASUALTY ALONE:** Watch their vital signs and make sure their condition improves.

—**GET OUT OF THE HEAT:** Reduce their exposure to heat in whatever way you can. Find a shady place or make something to provide shade.

—**COOL THE PATIENT:** Try to reduce their high internal temperature by applying damp compresses to their head, neck, groin and armpits. Improvise with clothing if compresses are not available. Try to cool them down by fanning them and by loosening their clothing. Avoid cooling them down to the point they get goosebumps or start to shiver.

—**MONITOR THEIR VITAL SIGNS:** Continue to monitor their breathing and consciousness. Make sure the relief from the heat and the provision of fluids is restoring their fluid balance.

—**GET MEDICAL HELP:** Heat stroke is a serious condition and the patient requires professional medical help. Depending on your situation, you may need to go for help, or you may have to consider carrying the casualty out.

HYPOTHERMIA

HYPOTHERMIA

Hypothermia occurs when your loss of heat is greater than your production of heat. Although there are different stages of hypothermia ranging from mild to severe, hypothermia is generally considered to occur when a person's core body temperature has decreased to 95°F / 35°C or less. The word "core" refers to your critical internal organs; in particular, your heart, brain, and lungs, while "periphery" or shell refers to your skin, muscles, and limbs. For your metabolism to function effectively, your core temperature must be maintained. At a temperature of 98.6°F / 37°C, your body functions normally. Below this temperature, chemical reactions begin to slow down. When your core drops to a temperature of 86°F / 30°C, or less, you have severe hypothermia, which is life threatening.

WHAT ARE THE HAZARDS OF HYPOTHERMIA?

Hazards range from light shivering to loss of mental and physical functioning to death. As your body temperature drops, biochemical processes slow down or become inefficient, affecting both your psychological and physiological functions. The drop in temperature causes different symptoms ranging from loss of coordination to mental deterioration.

Since hypothermia proceeds in stages, it is usually classified as impending, mild, moderate, and severe. The symptoms described below are only general signs of hypothermia and responses vary depending on factors such as age, health, and medication. In addition, hypothermia symptoms are classified slightly differently in different texts. Hypothermia actually occurs as a continuum of symptoms, and as such it is difficult to pinpoint exact discreet stages.

- **IMPENDING HYPOTHERMIA:** The body temperature has dropped from its normal 98.6°F / 37°C to 96.8°F / 36°C.

  —**SHIVERING:** The body starts to shiver to produce heat. At this stage, when hypothermia is only impending, victims can overcome shivering by increasing activity. Their pulse and breathing also increase.

  —**SKIN LOOKS PALE OR WAXY:** To reduce the loss of heat to the core, the body diverts blood from the extremities to the core. The surface of the skin cools causing it to look waxy.

  —**MUSCLES TENSE UP:** In response to the cold, muscles start to tense. However, this can be overcome by a gradual increase in activity, although the person may feel weak or fatigued.

- **MILD HYPOTHERMIA:** The body temperature has decreased to 93.2-95°F / 34-35°C.

  —**SHIVERING:** The person now has hypothermia, and the body tries to protect the core temperature by shivering. However, shivering is now intense and the person cannot overcome it by increasing activity.

  —**SKIN FEELS NUMB:** As blood is drawn away from the surface of the skin to conserve heat for the core through the process of vasoconstriction, the skin become cold, numb, or has goose bumps. Fingers are stiff and the afflicted person is unable to perform tasks with their hands. This is because the chemical reactions required to produce energy for muscular function do not work properly at these temperatures.

"The line between the shivering stage and the past shivering stage is gray. If the person is past the stage of being active, take action."

—Lloyd Gallagher

Hypothermia occurs when your loss of heat is greater than your production of heat.

—**RESPONSES ARE SLOW:** Although the person is still able to walk and talk, they exhibit inadequate responses such as failing to put on a wind-jacket or a hat. They may have difficulty completing complex motor activities such as skiing but do not generally recognize that they are hypothermic.

• **MODERATE HYPOTHERMIA:** The body temperature has decreased to 87.8-91.4°F / 31-33°C.

—**SHIVERING IS VIOLENT:** Shivering becomes more violent and intense as the body continues its attempts to produce heat.

—**MUSCLES ARE SLUGGISH:** As muscles stiffen, the person loses co-ordination, and has slow, labored movements, stumbles or is unable to use their hands.

—**APPEARS WITHDRAWN:** As mental deterioration sets in, the person exhibits sluggish thinking, appear withdrawn, apathetic or have difficulty speaking clearly.

• **SEVERE HYPOTHERMIA:** The body temperature is less than 87.8°F / 31°C.

—**SHIVERING STOPS:** The person displays bouts of shivering—shivering violently for a little while, and then stopping. Eventually, the shivering will stop entirely because the enzyme reactions that produce muscle contractions can no longer function. Since the core temperature is dropping, the body stops shivering to conserve heat. The person is in a "metabolic icebox."

—**MUSCLES BECOME RIGID:** As circulation slows down, waste products, called acid metabolites, begin to build up in the muscles of the extremities and the muscles stiffen.

"The water, opaque with glacial sediment and only a few degrees warmer than the ice it had so recently been, was the color of wet concrete."

—Jon Krakauer

HYPOTHERMIA
(continued)

—**SKIN MAY LOOK BLUE:** Since there is a lack of oxygen near the surface of the skin, lips and fingertips as well as the extremities or exposed skin might be blue in color.

—**PULSE AND BREATHING SLOW DOWN:** As a result of decreased chemical reactions, the body slows down, reducing the heart and breathing rate. The person may occasionally breathe, with gasps occurring at a rate of four or five per minute. The person may lie down on the ground and curl up in a fetal position.

—**MENTAL CONFUSION OR LOSS OF CONSCIOUSNESS:** As the vital organs cool, brain cell metabolism slows down causing brain function to become impaired. As a result, the person can become irrational, incoherent and eventually lose consciousness. Since the pupils can be dilated and fixed, and the pulse might not be detectable, the person appears to be dead.

Death occurs only when a person is warm and cardiac arrest cannot be reversed; thus the saying, "No one is dead until they are warm and dead." Above a core temperature of 77°F / 25°C, hypothermia alone may not be life threatening. However, cardiac arrest can only be reversed in a medical setting.

TIPS ON AVOIDING HYPOTHERMIA

Preventing hypothermia is much easier than treating hypothermia. Since hypothermia basically occurs when heat loss outweighs heat production, it can occur in the summer or winter, and in any terrain. The circumstances that contribute to getting hypothermia vary. They include personal as well as environmental factors. However, if you follow the tips below, you will greatly decrease your risk of getting hypothermia.

• **CREATE YOUR OWN MICRO-CLIMATE:** Take measures to prevent heat loss through conduction, convection, radiation, evaporation and respiration.

Tips for Keeping Warm at Night

Depending on what equipment you have, there are a few things you can do to keep warm.

• **Wear dry clothes:** Wet clothes conduct heat away from the body. If you have dry clothing, put it on. If you have a bivouac bag or garbage bag, stuff your wet clothes in the bottom. Your body heat may dry them by the morning. If you do not have many layers and need to wear all of your clothes, put your wet clothes on over your dry clothes.

• **Wear a hat:** Since you lose significant heat through your head, wear a hat. If you do not have one, wrap your head using whatever clothing you have. Covering your head makes a big difference in how warm you feel.

• **Warm up:** Move around a bit before going to bed. If you exercise a little, your muscles will warm up slightly and generate some heat. Avoid exercising so hard that you break a sweat since this causes you to lose heat.

• **Cuddle up:** If another person or a pet is there, cuddle up and share your warmth. If you have two sleeping bags, zip together and crawl in.

• **Have a hot drink:** If you have a stove or fire, make yourself a hot drink. Similarly, eating a snack gives an extra injection of energy.

• **Take a hot water bottle to bed:** If you can heat water, fill up your water bottle with hot water. Wrap it in a sock or other piece of clothing for insulation. Tuck it into your sleeping bag or bivouac bag.

—**DRESS IN LAYERS:** Instead of wearing one heavy layer that does not breathe or allow you to modify your clothing depending on your needs, adopt the layer approach. Layering enables you to take off or put on clothing as you require. It also prevents heat loss by evaporation.

—**WARD OFF THE COLD:** As soon as you start getting cold, put on another layer. This conserves what heat you have and prevents further heat loss. Make sure your clothes provide warmth and release moisture.

—**AVOID OVERHEATING:** If you work up a sweat, you will burn up energy and lose heat through excessive perspiration. Sweating accounts for two-thirds of your evaporative heat loss, while respiration accounts for the rest.

—**CONTROL BREATHING RATE TO REDUCE HEAT AND MOISTURE LOSS:** The higher your breathing rate, and the colder and drier the air, the greater the heat loss. If you work up a sweat in a cold environment, you will cool your body which contributes to heat loss. It will make your clothes wet which further conducts heat away from your body.

—**COVER YOUR MOUTH AND NOSE:** Since you lose heat by respiration, wear a facemask on really cold days.

HYPOTHERMIA
(c o n t i n u e d)

How the Body Loses Heat

People lose heat in five ways: radiation, conduction, convection, evaporation and respiration.

• **Radiation:** When the temperature of an object is higher than its surroundings, it emits energy as infrared radiation (heat). For example, at a normal body temperature of 98.6°F / 37°C, your skin radiates heat to the environment. Your head in particular radiates heat, throwing off about 35-50% of your total heat. This occurs because the blood vessels in the head, unlike the rest of the body, do not constrict. Since your head is such a good radiator of heat, wear a hat if you start to get cold.

• **Conduction:** When a warm object directly contacts a cold object, heat is transferred and lost through conduction. For example, you are cross-country skiing, and stop for lunch. Since there is nothing else to sit on, you sit on the snow. Soon, you begin to feel chilled, because your body heat is conducted to the cold snow. The amount of heat you lose is determined by factors such as the difference in temperature between the two objects (you and the snow); the surface area that acts as a conductor (the size or amount of your tush contacting the snow), and the effectiveness of the insulation (are you wearing a thin layer of cotton or several layers of polar fleece).

• **Convection:** When heat is transferred from a warm object to a cold object through moving air or water, it is lost through convection. When a cold wind blows across you, your heat is transferred to the air, warming the air, and cooling you. You lose the small micro-climate of air next to your body, which insulates you and keeps you warm.
Moving water causes you to lose heat by both conduction and convection. Immersing yourself in cold moving water can be an immediate threat to your temperature balance.

• **Evaporation:** When water evaporates from the surface of your body, heat is lost. Normally, about 20% of your heat is lost through the latent heat of evaporation. However, when you become too hot, you can lose much more heat through this process, possibly up to 1,000 calories per hour.

• **Respiration:** While people lose heat primarily through sweating, respiration is also a factor. When you inhale, air is warmed and humidified as it enters the lungs. When you exhale, moisture evaporates from the lungs and airways. Heat is lost in the process and your body cools (dogs in particular cool off through respiration.) In addition, sunburn also plays a role since it causes a loss in surface temperature regulation.

HYPOTHERMIA
(continued)

—BRING A HAT AND MITTENS: You lose significant heat by radiation especially from your head. If you are cold put on a hat. Mittens and socks do the same thing for your hands and feet.

—BRING A WINDPROOF LAYER: Standing on top of a windy ridge at minus 4°F / minus 20°C wearing only a layer of fleece will convince you of the advantages of a wind jacket and pants. If it is windy, or if you are cold, put on a windproof layer and get out of the wind. This prevents loss of heat through convection.

—REPLACE WET CLOTHES WITH DRY ONES: Since water conducts heat, wearing wet clothes could make you quite chilly. Some people take along an extra polypropylene or pile undershirt when they are in the backcountry. Once their shirt gets wet, they quickly take it off and change into a dry one. Try to change when you are in a sheltered place otherwise you may chill yourself further. Wearing dry clothes makes a big difference in temperature and comfort level. If you are still cold and need an additional layer, try placing your damp clothes over your dry ones as this will provide some insulation but you will not feel so damp.

—LOOSEN YOUR BOOTS: If your feet are cold, loosen your boots. This improves circulation and restores heat.

• **PREVENTING HEAT LOSS FROM A COLD ENVIRONMENT:** Aside from creating your own micro-climate, you can also create your own mini macro-climate by following the tips below.

—FIND OR MAKE SHELTER: If the weather turns and the temperature drops, seek shelter. If you can find a cabin, vehicle or other shelter, use it. Otherwise, find your own shelter. A dense clump of trees, a natural outcrop such as a rock, hill, or depression, a cave or the base of a large tree could offer protection from the wind and cold. You can also improvise and make your own shelter using whatever is handy such as tree trunks, boughs, fallen trees, blocks of snow, or a snow trench or snow cave.

"When I train people how to treat a person with hypothermia, I tell them to think of the person as a member of their family or their friend. If your loved one were severely hypothermic, would you give up? No, you would keep trying."

—Lloyd Gallagher

—INSULATE YOURSELF FROM THE GROUND: You lose significant heat through conduction by sitting on cold ground. Insulate yourself by using tree branches, a sleeping pad, your skis or your pack. If the ground is wet, sitting on it will create a further hazard since your clothes will get wet. Wet material conducts heat away from your body much more quickly than does dry material.

• **CREATE HEAT:** You can further modify your own environment by creating heat. Always carry a firestarter in your pack.

—BUILD A FIRE: A fire is an excellent source of heat, and you can make one in summer or winter if you have a fire starter. The dead lower branches of trees burn fairly easily as will the wood inside of fallen logs and tree bark.

—STOKE UP YOUR FURNACE: Eat high energy food containing fast burning carbohydrates such as nuts and granola. Drink hot fluids and move around. Keep your own heat-producing fires burning.

—SHARE YOUR HEAT: Huddle together with your friends and create a wind barrier for yourself. You could sit back to back or front to back, and you could also warm each others' hands or feet.

—**MOVE AROUND:** Your muscles account for half of your body weight and produce almost three quarters of your heat when they are working. If you are getting cold, do not stand still. Move around. However, exercise burns up calories so do not overdo it as you may end up depleting valuable energy reserves.

• **EXERCISE GOOD PERSONAL JUDGEMENT:** Avoid letting your desire to reach your destination overrule your judgement. If you are tired, or weather is moving in, take a few moments and evaluate your situation before continuing on.

—**SIT OUT BAD WEATHER:** If the weather turns nasty, consider staying where you are (if it is warm and dry) rather than pressing on despite all indications to the contrary. Perhaps the bad weather is temporary; you might only have to sit out a thunderstorm for an hour or two. Waiting and proceeding in dry weather rather than stoically forging ahead in a squall might be faster and safer in the long run.

—**ENJOY THE OUTDOORS WITHIN YOUR ABILITIES:** If you tackle a route that is too hard, you might find yourself stuck in the middle of nowhere with daylight fading and a storm approaching. That, together with little extra clothing, no food, and no fire starter could add up to hypothermia.

—**AVOID WAITING UNTIL YOU ARE REALLY COLD BEFORE YOU DO SOMETHING:** If your hands are cold put them in your armpits or your crotch where major arteries will help warm them. Ward off the danger that has not yet come.

—**WATCH OUT FOR YOUR FRIENDS:** As body temperature drops, mental deterioration follows. Since people with moderate to severe hypothermia do not have the mental acuity to look after themselves you have to look out for them.

—**BE AWARE OF THE SYMPTOMS OF MILD, MODERATE AND SEVERE HYPOTHERMIA:** Presence or absence of shivering, lack of co-ordination, and confusion are obvious flags. Remember, a hypothermic person is the last to realize they are in danger.

—**BE PREPARED:** Plan in advance for sudden changes in weather, bad weather, injuries, and accidents, all of which could contribute to hypothermia. If you leave your parka at home thinking that you will not need it, that is generally when something happens and you will wish you had it. Murphy's Law: Whatever you carry, you do not need. Whatever you leave at home, you need.

—**AVOID BECOMING EXHAUSTED:** Move at a comfortable pace that you can continue indefinitely. You cannot afford to get exhausted: Fatigue contributes to hypothermia as well as bad judgment.

TREATING HYPOTHERMIA

Since a reduction in core body temperature has both psychological and physiological affects, the hypothermic person usually becomes irrational or confused and does not recognize that she/he is hypothermic. If you suspect someone is developing hypothermia, look after it immediately. As it progresses, the condition becomes more serious and the treatment becomes more complicated. Use the following chart as a guideline for treating hypothermia.

HYPOTHERMIA
(continued)

"It's been years since I've worn cotton; it's like wearing a wet towel all day," explains a hypothermia survivor. *"Now I go overboard and carry two or three toques and I've always got a fleece undershirt along, even in the summer."*

—*Hypothermia Survivor*

CAUTION:

—**AVOID GIVING A HYPOTHERMIC PERSON ALCOHOL, CAFFEINE, OR NICO-TINE:** Since alcohol is a vasodilator, it increases surface blood flow and thus increases heat loss. Caffeine is a diuretic and increases dehydration. Nicotine, a vasoconstrictor, further decreases blood supply to the surface, increasing the risk of frostbite.

—**ASSUME SERIOUS HYPOTHERMIA IF YOU ARE UNSURE OF THE DEGREE OF SEVERITY:** Since you can endanger the person by providing the wrong treatment, assume the person has severe hypothermia and treat for it if you are uncertain. Otherwise, you may produce further complications or even death.

HYPOTHERMIA
(continued)

Treating Hypothermia

IMPENDING / MILD HYPOTHERMIA	SIGNS AND SYMPTOMS	TREATMENT
	• Person complains of being cold • Responds slowly • Shivers • Skin looks pale or waxy • Skin feels numb	• Get victim out of the cold • Replace wet clothing with dry clothing • Cover the head and neck • Stop further heat loss by providing extra clothes, a sleeping bag, or other insulation • Provide a warm drink or food if the victim is conscious and can swallow easily

MODERATE / SEVERE HYPOTHERMIA	SIGNS AND SYMPTOMS	TREATMENT
	· Violent shivering · Loss of coordination · Slurred speech · Mental confusion · Does not recognize that hypothermia is setting in As severity increases, the following can occur: • Shivering stops • Muscles get rigid • Pulse and breathing slow down • Victim loses consciousness	• Cover the victim to end exposure to the cold • Do not allow the victim to move • Avoid jostling the victim • Transport the victim to a medical facility where warming will take place. If the victim cannot be evacuated quickly, start rewarming the victim in the field. • Apply warmth to the head, neck, armpits, and groin in the form of a warm person, sleeping bag, or water bottle • Provide a warm drink or food only if the victim is fully conscious and can swallow easily

Left: Hypothermia can occour in the summer or winter, and in any terrain. It can also be prevented.

ICE

INSECT STINGS

ICE
(See WATER CROSSINGS)

INSECT STINGS (See "S" for SPIDERS)

Wasps, hornets, mosquitoes, and black flies are often present near forests and wetlands. If conditions are favorable, these pesky insects can appear in hordes. Wet areas such as marshes and shallow ponds are prime breeding sites for mosquitoes. Bees, wasps and hornets are drawn to meadows with an abundance of showy and fragrant wildflowers.

While black flies tend to swarm, other insects such as horse flies tend to attack people on a dive. Regardless of the type of insect, biting bugs leave some of their own bug saliva in people's skin. This causes immune systems to release histamines in an attempt at defense. The reaction can cause anything from temporary redness to significant swelling or even an anaphylactic shock reaction in allergic individuals. Some insects do not stop there. Black flies, for example, leave an anticoagulant that causes people's blood to flow more freely.

Research indicates that bugs are attracted to carbon dioxide, a gas people expel when they breathe out and perspire. Bugs are also attracted to movement. Bright fabrics, shiny jewelry, perfumed soap and fragrances also attract stinging insects. Leaving a delectable treat outside such as a slice of watermelon is another way to invite a crowd of hornets and other insects to a banquet. According to some studies, if people wave their hands in the air and slap their thighs in an attempt to ward off bugs, it only serves to attract them. Waving to beat off hornets only makes them more combative.

TIPS FOR CONTROLLING INSECT BITES

To reduce your attractiveness to the insect world, try wearing plain clothing instead of bright fabrics. Cover up by wearing long pants, a few layers of light clothing, or an outer layer of tightly woven fabric. Some outdoors stores sell hats with netting to prevent bothersome bites to your head and face.

Avoid wearing flowery perfumes, as this is only an invitation to a feast. Consider using an insect spray containing DEET (diethyltoluamide) to repel mosquitoes and other critters. As some people are allergic to DEET, apply a small amount first and see whether it causes a reaction such as swelling or redness. Some repellants can be sprayed on clothing instead of on the skin.

To reduce the severity of a reaction once you have been bitten, talk to a pharmacist or other medical professional about trying an over-the-counter antihistamine as this can reduce redness and swelling. Some lotions and salves, available over the counter, can also reduce swelling. Applying ice can reduce the diffusion of venom if it is applied within 10 minutes after being bitten. Cold compresses can also reduce itching.

Honeybees are the only insects that leave a venomous barb and venom sack in the skin after they sting. As the sack continues to throb, it injects more venom into the skin. If the barb or venom sack is visible, use a pair of tweezers to take it out.

Some people are more susceptible to insect bites and stings than others, although the reasons for this are not clear. Temporary redness, swelling and itching is common. However, symptoms such as fainting, shortness of breath, redness or other reactions throughout the body can indicate an allergic reaction. If you suspect such a reaction, get emergency care as soon as possible. Severe allergic reactions can be fatal in a matter of minutes. If you know you are allergic to insect bites, carry antihistamines with you. Some people even need

"I kind of like it when the natural world clobbers our technological universe. So what if hurricanes, earthquakes, mosquitoes, and idiot cattle make my life miserable? Thank God nature can still kick me and all my gadgets in the teeth."

—John Nichols

to carry a syringe of adrenaline. Train others how to administer the medication to you. If you have a severe reaction to a first bite, this could indicate you may have an even more severe reaction or have an anaphylactic shock reaction to a subsequent exposure.

LIGHTNING

Thunderclouds can bring heavy rain, hail and lightning. Lightning typically occurs in towering cumulonimbus clouds. As ice crystals and hailstones within the cumulonimbus cloud collide, they produce an electrical charge. The positive charges gather near the top of the cloud, while the negative ones gather near the bottom.

As the cloud travels above the surface of the ground, it becomes positively charged. An electrical field is created between the ground and the cloud, and the air begins to conduct electricity. This results in a massive discharge of high voltage electrical current known as lightening. A discharge from cloud to ground is called fork lightning while a discharge within the cloud or from cloud to cloud is called sheet lightning. In sheet lightning, part of the discharge channel is hidden by cloud. This makes the cloud appear to glow inside.

There are three other forms of lightning: St. Elmo's fire, ball lightning and rocket lightning. St. Elmo's fire appears as a glowing discharge around objects such as trees and hair. Ball lightning appears as a glowing sphere of air. Rocket lightning extends from the top of the cloud into the atmosphere instead of from the bottom of the cloud to the ground or from cloud to cloud.

LIGHTNING

FINDING SAFE PLACES IN A THUNDERSTORM

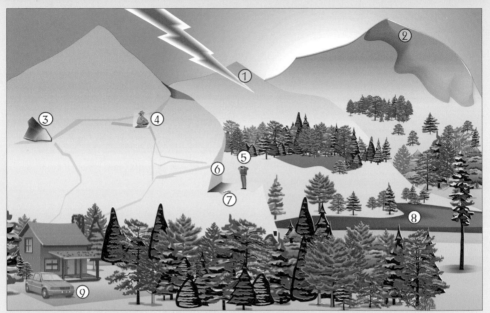

1. Since a lightning strike takes the shortest distance from cloud to ground, a mountain peak is an extremely hazardous location during a thunderstorm. Avoid projections such as peaks, ridge crests, rock spurs, high rocks and solitary tall trees.

2. Retreat from the summit as quickly as is safely possible. Even descending a few hundred feet / meters increases the margin of safety. If on a glacier, try to get off of it since you can become the high point.

3. Take shelter in deep caves located away from a high point. Avoid touching the walls. Make sure the cave is dry and large enough to keep you out of the rain.

4. If you have a pack, sleeping bag, or other insulator, put it on the ground and crouch on it. This insulates you from ground shock. Do not place your hands on the ground since electricity could pass through your hands and into your vital organs. Do not lie on the ground, since you then become a larger target. Instead of standing, which makes you a higher target, squat with your feet close together. Put your hands on your knees and your head between them. If you are in a group, do not huddle together. Spread apart. This makes the group a smaller target.

5. Find shelter near trees that are shorter than the ones surrounding them. Avoid tall, solitary trees.

6. Find a cliff to act as a lightning rod. Move well away from the cliff, since leaning against or near it exposes you to ground currents.

7. Although metal does not attract lightning, electrical currents can be induced in metal objects if they are near the strike zone. To avoid induced currents, place metal objects such as knives and ice axes well away from where you are. A charge from an induced current will be much less than that from a direct strike or ground currents.

8. When lightning strikes an object, it does not stop there but spreads out, traveling along the line of least resistance. The electricity flows along conductors such as lakes and hollows, streams and ditches, and overhangs and small caves. Avoid terrain that could conduct ground currents.

9. Seek shelter inside a building or vehicle. The electricity passes through the metal instead of the air, in a phenomenon known as the Faraday-cage effect.

WHERE DOES LIGHTNING STRIKE?

The light from flashes of lightning travels 186,000 miles / 297,000 kilometers per second while sound travels 1,083 feet / 330 meters per second. Count the seconds between seeing a flash of lightning and hearing a rumble of thunder. A five-second interval indicates a distance of about one mile / 1.6 kilometers.

Lightning seeks the path of least resistance to the ground. This is often, but not always, the shortest route. Projections such as mountain peaks, ridge crests, and rock spurs attract a direct lightning strike. A single tall tree can also receive a direct strike since it is the highest point on the horizon. If you stand on top of a peak or ridge crest during a thunderstorm, you become the highest point on the horizon. After lightning strikes, it does not stop but travels along the line of least resistance. Ground currents are strongest near the point at which the lightning struck. They decrease in intensity as they travel away from the strike.

Since water is a good conductor of electricity, ground currents may flow along damp cracks in the rock and wet gullies. Current may also travel along wet depressions in the rock or small concavities in cliffs. Mountain streams and lakes are good conductors as are water-saturated ditches and canyons. The current seeks the path of least resistance as it flows along. If there is a gap in the conductor, the electricity can arc from one conductor to another. If you are in a location that conducts electricity such as a small cave, the current can travel through you. Move away from these areas if you suspect lightning can occur. Although metal does not attract lightning, electrical currents can be induced in metal objects if they are near the strike. The intensity of a charge from an induced current is much less than from a direct strike or ground currents. Because of the risk of induced currents, shed any metal objects such as lighters, belt buckles or climbing gear as you can become burned. The electrical voltage across a lightening bolt may be 200 million to two billion volts. The high voltage can disrupt the electrical functioning of the brain and heart and produce a "flashover" effect in the person it strikes as it flows outside the body.

The heart recovers from the electrical shock more quickly than the brain. The person can stop breathing because the brain controls respiration. Although the heart recovers from the electrical shock more quickly than the brain and may resume beating on its own accord, it stops functioning because it needs oxygen too. Because of this, experts recommend artificial respiration as the most important first aid for lightning victims.

If a number of people are injured by lightning, first attend to people who have stopped breathing, have no pulse or who appear to be dead. Up to half an hour or more of artificial respiration can be required before the person resumes breathing. The seriousness of the injury is determined by a number of factors such as the parts of the body through which the current flowed and the strength of the current. A weak current can be fatal if it flows through the brain or affects vital organs such as the lungs and heart. A strong current inflicts less damage if it misses major organs.

SIGNS OF APPROACHING THUNDERSTORMS

• **SUDDEN TEMPERATURE CHANGES:** Rising wind and dropping temperatures precede a lightning strike. This results from a downburst of cold air that accompanies the thunderstorm.

• **IONIZATION OF AIR:** As the air becomes charged with electricity, it gives off a distinctive scent. It comes from ozone, a form of oxygen gas that has three atoms of oxygen instead of two. The air also begins to hum. Hair stands on end.

• **THUNDER:** When the air is suddenly heated, it expands and produces shock waves that create thunder.

L

LIGHTNING
(continued)

LOST

LOST

If you do get lost, you can increase your margin of safety by following these steps:

• **KEEP CALM:** If you get upset and act irrationally, you can make your situation much worse than it really is. The more you panic, the more problems you can create.

• **ASSESS YOUR PREDICAMENT:** Instead of rushing off in a panic, take a moment to analyze your situation. Are you hiking, cycling or skiing? How far away could you be from your starting point? What extra equipment do you have with you? Could you build a shelter and survive a night out?

• **CHECK THE MAP:** If you have a map and visibility is good, compare the features on the map with what you see around you. Find some distinguishing landmark such as a uniquely shaped peak and try to find out where you are.

• **USE YOUR GPS IF YOU HAVE ONE:** GPS is effective in pinpointing your location even in poor visibility.

• **MAKE A PLAN:** If you have momentarily lost your way because of poor weather, your best option might be to sit it out. Wait for the weather to clear and then try to identify your location. If you are not waiting out bad weather and cannot identify your location, you have two options: stay put, or move on.

STAYING PUT

• **IF YOU REALLY DO NOT KNOW WHERE YOU ARE, STAY WHERE YOU ARE:** Searchers will find you more quickly if you do not wander around. If you told someone where you were going before you left, you have the added psychological advantage of knowing someone will search in the area you identified.

• **MAKE YOURSELF VISIBLE:** Use whatever is available in your pack or your surroundings to make your location apparent to searchers. If you are in bush, try to find a clearing. Spread brightly colored clothing on the ground where people might see it from the air or use whatever objects are available to make your location visible. If you have flares and hear a plane or helicopter, shoot the flares before the helicopter is overhead.

• **STAY WARM AND DRY:** If you have to spend a night out, make some kind of shelter and wear all of your extra clothing. Make a fire if possible and guard against hypothermia.

MOVING ON

• **IF YOU DECIDE TO MOVE ON, MARK YOUR PRESENT LOCATION:** If you become even more lost when you move on, try to re-trace your steps back to location. At that point, either stay put and wait for help, or move on again, but this time in a different direction. Retrace your steps to your original location if you become lost in that direction.

MOOSE

Attaining a height of 6 feet / 2 meters or higher, the moose is chocolate brown in color and is the largest member of the deer family. Bulls weigh about 900 pounds / 409 kilograms while females are slightly smaller. This massive animal is easily identifiable by its large bulbous nose and the flap of skin dangling from its neck. It also has a large shoulder hump. Moose do not have a white rump patch, as do other members of the deer family. This animal is the second largest in North America (bison are the largest).

In the Algonkian language, the word "moose" means "twig eater." It is an appropriate name because this animal browses on willows and aspen found in mixed conifer and hardwood forests. Moose are good swimmers and can dive about 14 feet / 4 meters in search of aquatic vegetation to graze on. They are found near subalpine meadows and marshes. A moose's long legs allow it to

M O O S E

SURVIVING A NIGHT IN THE WOODS

1. Find an open place where people looking for you can see you easily. Make a sign using rocks or branches to show them where you are. Wear something bright if you can. This helps people see you.

2. Hug a tree near the open place. Staying in one place helps people find you quickly. Hugging a tree also helps you stay dry if it rains or snows. Put your hat and extra clothes on. Zip up your jacket. Snuggle up to your friend or pet. This keeps both of you warm and safe.

3. Make yourself a bed of boughs and branches or other material. This protects you from the cold ground. Make yourself comfortable and wait for searchers to find you. This helps you keep your energy and stop from worrying about what to do.

M O O S E
(continued)

move through deep snow in the winter. Despite its ungainly appearance, these massive animals can gallop at a speed of up to 35 MPH / 56 kph. However, they usually walk. Moose trot when in haste.

In April, mature males begin to develop velvet-covered antlers, which can grow to a width of 80 inches / 203 centimeters. They drop these antlers each year in the early spring. The mating season occurs in the fall. During the rut, bull moose are especially belligerent. If approached, a bull may regard a person as a potential suitor. In its quest for dominance, a bull may charge people as well as other animals and vehicles. Bull moose are extremely dangerous at this time and can strike out with hooves and antlers.

The calves are born about eight months later

Moose, like all wildlife, should be viewed from a respectable distance.

in late May to early June. Twins are uncommon: a cow usually bears one calf. A cow is very protective of its young especially during the first month. It may charge anything it perceives to be a threat such as an unwary hiker. Both sexes are short-tempered and also unpredictable. Although moose have poor eyesight, they defend themselves against predators such as wolves and mountain lions with their immense size and good sense of smell.

AVOIDING ENCOUNTERS WITH MOOSE

• **IF YOU SEE A MOOSE WHILE YOU ARE ON A TRAIL, MAKE WAY FOR THE MOOSE:** Retreat slowly and give it plenty of room to maneuver.

• **EXERCISE SPECIAL CAUTION DURING THE FALL RUTTING SEASON AND THE SPRING CALVING SEASON:** Do not approach a bull moose as it might regard you as a suitor. Do not approach a cow as it will view you as a threat to its calf.

• **AVOID GETTING BETWEEN A COW AND HER CALF:** Moose mothers are very protective, especially during the spring calving season.

• **IF YOU SEE A MOOSE WHILE YOU ARE DRIVING IN YOUR VEHICLE AND CHOOSE TO STOP, STAY IN YOUR VEHICLE:** View moose from the relative safety of your vehicle.

Moose Track

Mountain lions are solitary animals and do not usually approach people. But if you encounter a mountain lion, always face it instead of turning around and running.

MOUNTAIN LION

Variously called a mountain lion, cougar, panther, or puma, the mountain lion belongs to the family *Felidae*. It is the largest cat in North America. Described as *Felis concolor*, or "cat of one color," the mountain lion is generally tawny, although its kittens are spotted until about six months of age. Solitary and cautious, the adult male mountain lion measures almost 6.5 feet / 2 meters in length, not counting its long tail. Lighter on the sides than on the top, the mountain lion has a characteristic black spot above each eye.

A mountain lion weighs about 90-110 pounds / 40-50 kilograms. Its head is proportionately smaller than the rest of its body. Females are generally about 25-30% smaller than males. A consummate climber, mountain lions can jump from a height of 60 feet / 18 meters. Except when it is climbing, grasping prey, or accelerating, a mountain lion's claws are retracted. When young, a mountain lion plays with its siblings and cooperates in its budding hunting ventures. When it gets older however, the mountain lion remains solitary except when it is breeding.

Unlike bears, mountain lions are primarily predators hunting deer, sheep, and elk, as well as smaller animals. Although mountain lions were once widely distributed throughout the Western Hemisphere and adapted to desert, plains and mountains, their distribution is now primarily limited to the mountainous areas of Canada and to the western United States. They favor the foothills and montane life zones especially if there are large populations of prey such as deer, elk or bighorn sheep. However, these big cats do venture into the subalpine and alpine life zones during the summer in search of prey.

Encounters between mountain lions and people in the states of southern California, eastern Colorado and western Texas prompted a comprehensive study of mountain lion attacks in the United States and Canada to be undertaken. The overall objective was to study historical information in order to find ways to improve public safety.

The study, done by Paul Beier of the University of California, Berkeley, looked at all attacks involving people and mountain lions from 1890 to 1990. On the basis of this comprehensive work, Beier concluded the number of at-

M

MOUNTAIN
LION

Mountain Lion
Tracks

tacks on people did increase markedly in the last 20 years of the study period. More attacks occurred in those two decades than the sum of the first six. At the same time, the number of mountain lions and the number of people invading mountain lion habitat also increased.

Yearlings and mountain lions that were underweight were most likely to attack. Children, aged five to nine, were most likely to be attacked. Beier also noted that people could dispel an imminent attack or one that was happening by acting aggressively.

Beier points to a mountain lion attack that occurred in Boulder, Colorado. When two mountain lions approached a woman, she tried to deter them by standing her ground, waving her arms and shouting. However, when the animals continued to advance, she climbed a tree. The mountain lions climbed after her, one of them clawing her leg. She then hit one lion with her foot and the other with a stick. At that point, the animals descended from the tree and subsequently left the area.

Although Beier's landmark research has clarified our understanding of mountain lions and their behavior, one large question remains. Why are attacks on people increasing? Martin Jalkotzy, who studied mountain lions for 12 years in the Sheep River Area of Kananaskis Country, Canada, and who contributed to Beier's study, offers some insights into this complex question. "The reason you most often hear is that more of us are living in mountain lion habitat and the number of mountain lions are increasing so encounters are bound to increase," says Jalkotzy. "But we do not know if there really are more mountain lions since field surveys have not been done."

He points to recorded sightings as an example. As part of his study, Jalkotzy studied information from Banff National Park, Jasper National Park, and Waterton Lakes National Park from 1980 to 1990. "The recorded sightings were not restricted simply to visual sightings," he explains. "They included other indications such as tracks, vocalizations, kills made by mountain lions, and traffic accidents involving them. "

Because it was not possible to check the accuracy of these sightings, Jalkotzy accepted them all as valid for the purpose of his study. On the basis of this and other information, he notes there was an apparent increase in sightings in Banff and Jasper National Park between 1980 and 1990. It is only "apparent" because the sightings could not be verified.

Jalkotzy says it is also not possible to conclude this increase proves there is an increase in the number of mountain lions or that their distribution is changing. "It may point more to a change in the patterns of people visiting the parks," he explains. "And if there are more of us in the bush, perhaps we will report seeing them more often."

Jalkotzy says life-threatening attacks on people do not happen often. However, information from the United States (for example, Boulder, Colorado, and Big Bend National Park, Texas) and Canada (for example, Waterton Lakes National Park) show the number and types of attacks that occur in these two countries are similar.

What can decrease the probability of an attack? Jalkotzy believes the question of whether hunting reduces encounters between the big cats and a person is not relevant. "The result may be fewer mountain lions but we do not know whether that would reduce attacks," he explains. "Hunting has nothing to do with improving public safety really."

He points to Vancouver Island. At one point, there was a bounty on mountain lions in that area. At the same time, there were more attacks there than

People who live near mountain lion habitat—such as Boulder, Colorado—learn to co-exist with the native resident.

anywhere else in North America. "None of the information suggesting hunting mountain lions decreases attacks on people is plausible," Jalkotzy points out.

As for his own experience, Jalkotzy was only attacked once in his 12 years of studying these big cats. It occurred in an area where a mountain lion had killed a mule deer doe—a potentially dangerous situation.

He also says that simply seeing a mountain lion is a rare event. One of the ways he got a glimpse into the lives of these big cats was by looking for their tracks in the snow. Once the new tracks were identified, he would backtrack—follow the tracks back in the direction from which they came. This enabled him to study the movements of the mountain lion without disturbing it. Researchers only follow tracks forward when they are certain the animal is no longer in the area. Jalkotzy admires the secretive animals that he describes as "phantoms." "They are there and then they are not," he explains.

The consultant believes people are at much greater risk when driving down the highway than when traveling in mountain lion habitat. "We do not normally report all of the grisly details of car accidents in the newspapers," he explains, "but when an attack between a mountain lion and a person or a bear and a person occurs, it makes the front page. Man's best friend, the dog, is responsible for maiming and killing more people in North America each year than all of the combined attacks by wildlife."

AVOIDING ENCOUNTERS WITH MOUNTAIN LIONS

• **IF YOU SEE A MOUNTAIN LION IN THE DISTANCE, AVOID IT:** Do not succumb to your curiosity and follow a desire to check it out. A mountain lion is elusive and will likely run off if it sees you. If it does not, it could have a reason to stay in your vicinity. For example, there might be a carcass nearby and it could become a source of conflict between you and the mountain lion.

• **A MOUNTAIN LION IS LESS LIKELY TO STALK A LARGE GROUP THAN A SINGLE PERSON:** In addition, you have a better chance of protecting yourself in a group. Avoid walking alone if you are in an area where mountain lions are a concern.

MOUNTAIN
LION
(continued)

• **MAKE LOTS OF NOISE WHEN YOU TRAVEL:** This alerts the mountain lion of your presence and gives it an opportunity to run off before you come along.

• **MOUNTAIN LIONS MAY BE AGGRESSIVE WITH DOGS:** In Waterton Lakes National Park, Alberta, mountain lions have taken dogs within sight of their owners. Although a pack of six to eight dogs can frighten and tree a mountain lion, these big cats are not afraid of dogs on a one-to-one basis. Mountain lions, in particular sub-adult animals who have been displaced into towns, will go after small dogs and cats as food. In a dog/mountain lion conflict, the dog generally loses. And a mountain lion can chase a dog back to its owner, increasing the chance of a human/mountain lion conflict. When traveling in the backcountry or in mountain lion habitat, keep your dog on a leash. If you live in mountain lion habitat, leave your pet in a secure kennel. A secure top could prevent a mountain lion attack. Bring your pet into your house at night if the kennel is not secure.

• **KEEP YOUR CHILDREN BESIDE YOU WHEN TRAVELING IN MOUNTAIN LION HABITAT**: Avoid allowing them to wander off unattended into the bush where they can meet a mountain lion. Dense vegetation provides ideal cover for a mountain lion. If a mountain lion sees a small child playing alone, and especially crawling along the ground, it might mistake your child for a prey animal. You can reduce this risk by having your child play in a group. Have your child stay well away from dense foliage where a mountain lion might be hiding. Similar to deer, their primary prey, mountain lions are not nocturnal. They are most active about two to three hours before and after sunrise or sunset. They are less active at midday and in the middle of the night. Talk to your children about mountain lions. Tell them how to avoid close encounters.

• **MOUNTAIN LION PREY ON ANIMALS SUCH AS DEER, MOUNTAIN SHEEP, ELK, AND SMALLER ANIMALS:** If you feed or attract these animals, you can attract a mountain lion too. If you live in mountain lion habitat, consider whether your lawn and garden might attract mountain lions. If your yard is lush and full of foliage, mule deer will be attracted and so will mountain lions.

MANAGING A CLOSE ENCOUNTER WITH A MOUNTAIN LION

You can help prevent an incident from turning into an attack by having a basic understanding of mountain lion behavior and following a few guidelines.

Mountain lions prey on animals much larger than themselves such as mule deer, elk, and bighorn sheep. Their "prey image" is an animal on four legs—not an animal on two legs that walks upright. Avoid crouching down or allowing small children to crawl around unattended when in mountain lion habitat. However, a small crawling child or a crouching adult does fit the mountain lion's prey image and could provoke aggressive behavior on the part of the lion.

Try to stay calm since many encounters between people and mountain lions result in the mountain lion walking away. Since mountain lions are predators and often seize their prey at the back of the neck, do not turn and run away. Instead, stand tall and face the mountain lion at all times. Since a small child can look like a prey animal to a mountain lion, immediately pick him/her up. The quick movements of a child could excite a mountain lion. Have larger children stand behind you. Always facing the mountain lion, back away slowly. If you are attacked or if a mountain lion persists in stalking you, attempt to deter it. Shout, wave a stick, or throw rocks at the mountain lion.

MUDSLIDES

MUDSLIDES

A mudslide or debris flow occurs when the surface of a slope collapses quickly and slides downward. Although mudslides can result from environmental catastrophes such as a volcanic eruption or earthquake, they are more often triggered by an accumulation of water. Long periods of excessive rainfall that saturate the ground, followed by short intense bursts of rainfall are thought to play a major role in the occurrence of mudslides.

Since mudslides result from a number of complex factors, it is difficult to predict when and where they will occur. Shallow flows, which occur in loose material such as colluvium and sand, gather speed quickly. They are more dangerous than deeper flows, which occur in more stable soils such as clay, and move more slowly. As the mudslide flows down the slope, it tears out obstructions in its path such as boulders and trees. Even a shallow mudslide, only a few feet deep, can result in a debris pile that weighs several tons.

• **BE AWARE OF SLOPES THAT COULD SLIDE**: If you are in the backcountry, be alert for conditions that could produce mudslides such as excessive or prolonged rainfall. Try to identify slopes that could slide, and avoid these areas. Steep slopes, especially ones devoid of vegetation, could have been produced by mudslides. Rounded slopes are often produced by an accumulation of soil and vegetation and can be less likely to slide.

• **LOOK FOR EVIDENCE OF PREVIOUS MUDSLIDES:** This includes narrow gullies found on the sides of hills. If a slope has slid before, it will likely slide again, although it is difficult to predict when this will happen. In addition, vegetation can quickly grow over a shallow mudslide and cover signs of its passing.

• **BE AWARE OF SIGNS OF AN APPROACHING MUDSLIDE:** In the mountains, you can gain some warning of an approaching mudslide by staying alert for certain signs. For example, the ground at the base of a slope can begin to swell. Cracks can appear in the ground, and can slowly become wider and wider. Water can surge out of the ground in places it has never erupted before. Natural objects that were previously stable such as trees can tilt or even begin to move. The ground can start to creep in a specific direction. You could feel the ground move underneath your feet, and you may hear a far-off rumbling sound that gains in intensity as the mudslide draws closer.

• **IF YOU ARE CAUGHT IN THE MOUNTAINS DURING A MUDSLIDE:**

—Climb to higher ground as quickly as possible.

—When the mudslide stops, keep away from the area that has slid as it may slide again. Also be aware that floods may occur after a mudslide.

—If you cannot get away from the path of the mudslide, take cover under the nearest shelter such as a large group of trees or a building such as a camp shelter. Curl up into a ball and try to protect your head by placing your hands and arms over it.

MULE DEER

MULE DEER

A member of the deer family, *Cervidae*, mule deer can be distinguished from white-tailed deer by their larger, mule-like ears for which they are named, as well as their larger eyes and their narrow, black-tipped white tail. The mule deer's chin and throat is white in color. While mule and white-tailed deer are about the same size, they are both smaller than elk and have smaller antlers.

Mule deer graze on a variety of grasses and wildflowers in the summer and browse on twigs and buds in the winter. They favor foothills, meadows with brush and montane forests. Mule deer, similar to wapiti (elk), are shy in the backcountry. However, they can become habituated to people. In some mountain parks, mule deer can be seen in campgrounds, along roadsides, or in people's yards eating the shrubbery.

Although they appear harmless, mule deer can be a hazard to people. When people feed them by hand, they can become dangerous, impatiently pawing their providers. If they do not get what they want, mule deer can become frustrated; striking out with their front hooves and inflicting bruises and cuts. These placid-looking animals can also strike with their antlers.

If people leave food around, the deer will eat it. They get used to human food and start feeding off picnic tables or even licking the grease from fire grates or barbecues. Mule deer can aggressively approach tables with food on them or approach people who are nearby. By feeding the deer, people make the problem worse and increase the hazard especially for children. Mule deer are sometimes belligerent in the backcountry and chew packs and clothing.

Since some mule deer are habituated to traffic, they may react unpredictably. Male mule deer (bucks) weigh about 160 pounds / 73 kilograms while females (does) weigh about 130 pounds / 60 kilograms. Colliding with a deer can cause serious damage to both people and their vehicles.

Similar to elk, mule deer breed during the fall and can become more aggressive at this time. Although mule deer do not bugle like elk, they do engage in "horning," which serves a similar purpose: A buck rubs his antlers against a tree or bush, making loud clacking sounds, which advertises his presence to other males in the area. Once they locate each other, they fight for the right to mate with the does. Although some matches are no more than a display of force and a retreat, bucks do spar. They engage their antlers, trying to knock their opponents off balance, and sometimes goring them.

AVOIDING ENCOUNTERS WITH MULE DEER

• **KEEP YOUR CAMPSITE CLEAN:** If you see mule deer around the park or at your campsite, resist feeding them. Although they look harmless, mule deer are wild animals.

• **EXERCISE CAUTION IF YOU SEE MULE DEER GRAZING ALONG THE SIDES OF HIGHWAYS AND DITCHES.** They may act unpredictably.

• **LEASH YOUR DOG:** To avoid a potential encounter between a mule deer and your dog, keep your dog on a leash and keep it well away from deer. Even if the deer is not provoked, it might still strike out at the dog.

• **BE ESPECIALLY WARY DURING MATING SEASON:** Avoid bucks especially during the fall rut, and does during the spring calving season.

Mule DeerTrack

Although they appear harmless, mule deer can become habituated to people and lose their fear of them.

NIGHTFALL

NIGHTFALL

When night falls, it is often better to stay put and find shelter rather than continue. Darkness obscures the route and leads to a myriad of hazards such as getting lost or succumbing to hypothermia. If you carry basic survival equipment and build a primitive shelter, a night out can result in little more than discomfort.

Try to find shelter an hour or so before night falls. Daylight or dusk gives you the light you need to search for a natural shelter or construct a primitive one. You can also feel psychologically more comfortable if you have constructed a shelter before dark falls. In addition, if the weather is deteriorating, find shelter before it hits full force. It is harder to make a shelter in driving rain than in clear weather and you will get wet making it. Find shelter before you become exhausted. If you push yourself to the limit, you will have less energy to make a shelter. Your judgement can suffer and things seem more difficult than they really are. And when you do built your shelter, conserve your energy. Try not to work up a sweat or tire yourself out as you build.

Your shelter should do two things: Protect you from the elements and prevent heat loss. The materials you use depend on whether it is summer or winter, what materials are available, and what survival gear you are carrying. Make sure you have chosen a site that is free from objective hazards such as rockfall and avalanches.

- **INSULATE YOURSELF FROM THE GROUND:** Since contacting cold ground causes you to lose heat through conduction, insulate yourself from it. Use a foamy ensolite, and your pack, tree boughs, equipment or whatever else you can find.

"At risk of a late return he pressed on, deeper into the wild silence, the monstrous and the menacing, despite that gathering darkness..."

—Thomas Mann

105

BUILDING SHELTERS

1. During winter, trees often have a dry pocket at their base because the boughs prevent snow from drifting in. Using a shovel, snowshoes, or your hands, dig out enough snow so you can crawl in and huddle up against the tree. Use boughs to insulate you from the cold ground. Create a roof using garbage bags, boughs or other materials.

2. To make a snow cave, find a moderately angled snow bank or slope. Using a shovel, snowshoe, other tool, or your hands, dig out a space about the size of your body. Tunnel up towards the back so the sleeping area is higher than the entrance. Since cold air is heavier than warm air, it drops towards the entrance, keeping your sleeping area warm. Using a stick or ski pole, make a

small opening for ventilation. Mark the snow cave on the outside using your skis, boughs, or other material so people can locate you. Using a snow block, pack, or tree boughs, seal the entrance.

3. To make a powder snow shelter, follow these steps:

—Find or make a couple of sticks about a body-length long. Drive one of the sticks into the snow so it stands vertically. This stick marks the center of your snow shelter. Using the second stick, draw a large circle around the vertical stick. This marks the diameter of your shelter. Place the second stick on the ground so one end touches the center stick and the other end reaches the outside perimeter of the shelter.

—Using a shovel, pot, or other implement, pile snow in the center of the shelter. As you pile the snow, pat it down to compact it. Continue piling snow until the center stick is covered. By this time, the mound will be about 6.5 feet / 2 meters high and about 12 feet / 4 meters wide. Let it sit for about three hours or longer. Give the snow time to compact. The longer you leave it, the more compact it becomes.

—Using the horizontal stick as a guide, dig out the shelter. Start at the end of the stick and keep shoveling until you reach the center. This is hot, sweaty, work. Tunnel out an entrance that is lower than the sleeping area. Since warm air rises, and cold air sinks, the cold air will sink to the doorway. Dig out the sides

BUILDING SHELTERS

Lightweight portable shelters can be used in a variety of situations and environments.

and top leaving the walls about a foot in width. If the snow looks translucent or light shines through, you have dug out too much. Insulate the sleeping area with boughs, foams, or packs. Pull out the center stick. The opening left by the stick provides ventilation. Seal the opening with packs, skis, or a tarp to prevent cold air from seeping in. Light a candle. This provides light and glazes the walls.

4. A dense stand of trees offers some cover from wind and the elements. Large trees with boughs that spread out widely and reach the ground may have dry ground underneath them.

5. Use the natural features of your environment to construct a shelter. Caves protect you from the wind, sun and rain. Rock outcrops often have three walls and offer similar protection to a cave. They may have a natural crawl space underneath them that may be dry. You can stuff openings in rock outcrops with moss, grass, small rocks or snow to stop the wind from blowing through.

6. Bring a portable shelter such as several heavy-duty garbage bags. They help protect you from wind as well as rain and snow. Portable shelters also provide some insulation. Use them along with other types of shelters such as a snow trench.

7. Bring along a fire starter so you can make a fire even during winter. The fire will provide warmth. You can also make two fires and sleep between them.

8. Make a snow trench. To do this, first dig out a trench about the size of your body or slightly larger. Angle the walls so the bottom of the trench is larger than the top. This gives you more room to lie down and creates a smaller roof to cover. Pile blocks of snow around the top of the trench to create short walls. These act as a windbreak. Create a roof using whatever material you have such as tree boughs, a tarp, garbage bags, and skis. Secure the roof by placing snow around the sides. Insulate the floor with boughs, moss, your pack, or foams.

As conditions in the mountains can change rapidly, travelers in the high country should be prepared to make shelter under a

NIGHTFALL
(continued)

• **PROTECT YOURSELF FROM THE WIND:** Wind robs you of heat by blowing away the warm air next to your skin. Make a shelter that is windproof or wind-resistant. Natural shelters such as caves and dense stands of trees offer some wind protection. So do portable shelters such as tent sacks. If you surround yourself with a portable shelter such as a bivouac sac or a natural shelter such as a snow cave, your body heat will gradually warm it up.

Wilderness Survival:

Ron Hood, of Hoods Woods, a wilderness survival company says the Tubatlabal of California often used a technique in the Sierra Mountains called the firebed. "I've used this on nights down to 0°F / -18°C," he explains.

Use the "rule of two, four, and eight—a two-hour burn, four inches (10 cm) of dirt covering, and an eight-inch (8.5 cm) deep hole." Caution: Avoid building:
—In a drainage area if possible
—On very wet soil, since it will steam you during the night and leave you with a "dishpan body"
—Over the root systems of trees.

1. Make a trench:
—Select a protected site with dry soft soil, sand, or dirt near a rock or under a metamorphic rock overhang. Make sure there is nothing nearby that could start a fire such as overhanging vegetation, sandstone, or composite rocks.
—Dig a hole about one foot wide and eight inches deep. Make it as long as you require, probably about five to six feet.
—Pile the dirt on the sides of the trench.
—Place small stones on the bottom of the trench. Although the stones don't hold much heat,

they bring air to the bottom of the fire. Avoid using stones from a stream since they may explode. Using larger stones has no appreciable effect on the release of heat.

variety of conditions. Portable and natural shelters can help you retain body heat and reduce the risks of exposure.

• **THERE ARE TWO MAIN TYPES OF SHELTERS—PORTABLE AND NATURAL:** A portable shelter is a lightweight shelter you can carry with you such as heavy-duty plastic garbage bags, a bivouac sac or a space blanket. Natural shelters are made from materials in your environment such as caves, outcrops, trees, and tree wells, or even snow.

NIGHTFALL
(continued)

Making a California-Style Firebed

2. Build a fire:
—Put fuel such as grass, tinder, and dead wood into the trench and light a fire.
—Keep an active fire burning. Spread the coals evenly as the fire burns.
—After about an hour and a half, let the fire drop to coals.
—When the fire has died, build a small fire nearby to provide you with light and warmth.

3. Fill the trench:
—Fill the firepit with the dirt that you piled on the sides of the trench. Ensure that every part of the trench is covered with at least

four inches of dirt. "Any less, and you will barbecue your butt," explains Hood.
• Allow the ground to heat up. After about 45 minutes, the earth will be warm and the surface will be moist.
—Check for any loose embers and discard any that you find.
—Cover the warm earth with available material such as leaves or pine needles. If you have plastic or garbage bags, place them over the earth to protect you from moisture seeping up from the ground. Getting into two garbage bags—one for your feet and lower body, and the other for

your upper body—keeps out moisture and helps retain heat.
—Go to sleep. If you get cold on top, roll over.

4. Restore the site:
—In the morning, scatter the pine needles or other debris that you used to as ground cover, and all traces of the firebed will disappear. The firebed is actually extinguished, when you place dirt on top of the fire. However, the soil retains heat and is gradually released throughout the night, which creates a warmth-generating bed for you.

P O I S O N O U S
P L A N T S

P O R C U P I N E S

POISONOUS PLANTS

The Rocky Mountains are rich in plant life. They contain thousands of species including trees, grasses, herbs, and lichens. Throughout the human history of the Rockies, plants have provided a rich array of foods. Native peoples of both the United States and Canada have also used wild mountain plants in making traditional medicines. However, many of these plants are also poisonous. For example, eating the bulb of the elegant looking herb, Mountain Death Camus, can be fatal. It contains a substance called zygadenine, which some researchers believe is more toxic than strychnine. In addition, this herb can easily be confused with edible herbs such as wild onions. Some of the more common poisonous plants are listed below. Because of the toxicity of wild plants, use a good field guide to identify and avoid them.

- **BLACK HENBANE:** Black henbane belongs to the nightshade family. Identified by its bell-shaped flowers, ragged leaves and unpleasing scent, black henbane is poisonous.

- **DEVIL'S CLUB:** Found in forested areas and foothills, the stems of devil's club are covered with poisonous spines that cause inflammation upon contact. The large, notched leaves of this plant are similar to those of the non-poisonous cow parsnip.

- **DEATH CAMAS:** As its name suggests, the bulb of death camas is highly poisonous. This plant can be distinguished from the less poisonous white camus by its flowers. The flowers of the death camas are smaller and placed more closely together on the spike than those of the more common death camus.

- **POISON IVY:** Brushing against poison ivy produces an unpleasant rash especially if you are very sensitive to it. You can identify this plant by its dark green leaves, which occur in clusters of three, the reddish color of the stems at junctions, and the clumps of small green flowers. White berries adorn this plant in the fall.

- **STINGING NETTLE:** Avoid touching the leaves of stinging nettle. The tiny spines in its leaves break off in your skin and cause it to become inflamed. This plant is similar in appearance to wild mint; however, while wild mint has an odor of mint, stinging nettle does not.

- **WATER HEMLOCK/WATER PARSNIP:** Found in boggy areas, water hemlock has clusters of small white flowers. The roots and lower parts of this plant are quite poisonous. Water parsnip, which looks similar, is also poisonous but not as toxic as water hemlock.

- **MUSHROOMS:** Although many mushrooms are edible, others are toxic. Since there are so many different varieties, do not eat them unless you are absolutely certain they are edible. Some of the toxic mushrooms include Fly agaric, poison pie, panther agaric, and emetic russula.

- **TALL LARKSPUR/MONKSHOOD:** Tall larkspur, found in subalpine meadows, is easy to identify by its spikes of deep blue or purple flowers. Although it is beautiful, it is also poisonous. Monkshood, similar in size and shape but not in flower, can be found growing along side of it. This plant is also poisonous.

Devil's Club

Do not approach a porcupine too closely; it might throw its quills if alarmed.

PORCUPINES

Porcupines belong to the rodent family and are the second largest rodent after beavers. They are about the size of a volleyball or larger and weigh about 10-20 pounds / 4.5-9 kilograms. Porcupines have a small black face and a short flat tail. They are often found in the subalpine life zone where they climb coniferous trees in search of food. Resting upon branches, this rodent can stay in a tree for days, consuming the cambium layer beneath the bark. A pile of twigs with the bark chewed off dropped at the base of a tree indicates the presence of a porcupine.

About 30,000 quills cover this large rodent. Hollow and sharp, the quills cover most of its body with the exception of the porcupine's legs, tail and face. When threatened, the porcupine retreats and protects its head and exposed parts by snuggling into a sheltered area. The quills swell and cover its feet. The tail moves back and forth ready to throw quills if the threat continues.

PORCUPINES AND PETS

Here are a few pointers on handling pet and porcupine encounters.

• **IF YOUR DOG GETS A FACE FULL OF QUILLS, EITHER PULL THE QUILLS OUT YOURSELF OR TAKE THE ANIMAL TO A VET AS SOON AS POSSIBLE:** Once in, the quills continue to work their way in. The longer you wait, the more serious the problem becomes. Since it is difficult to remove the quills by hand (although it can be done), carry a pair of pliers along with you for this purpose. Depending on the location of the quills, you can either pull or push them out.

• **IF YOU TAKE THE QUILLS OUT YOURSELF, TAKE YOUR DOG TO A VET AS SOON AS YOU CAN AFTERWARD:** You might miss some of the quills and they may become embedded. The dog may also eat any remaining quills and perforate its stomach in the process.

PORCUPINES
(continued)

RABIES

• **TO AVOID THIS UNPLEASANT EXPERIENCE IN THE FUTURE, KEEP YOUR DOG ON A LEASH WHILE IN THE BACKCOUNTRY:** A dog can become blinded by an encounter with a porcupine if the quills are driven into its eyes. In addition, if its mouth is full of quills, it is difficult for the dog to drink or eat and so it can starve if not looked after quickly.

PORCUPINES AND PEOPLE

Porcupines are attracted to salt. They chew away at salt on boots and clothing and the straps of packs and other equipment. Porcupines have also been known to drag these items away for future banquets.

• **TO AVOID LOSING YOUR BOOTS OR OTHER SALTY ITEMS TO A PORCUPINE, KEEP YOUR BOOTS INSIDE YOUR TENT:** Instead of leaving your pack or other equipment on the ground where resourceful porcupines could get at them, suspend them inside the tent or from two trees.

• **THESE LARGE RODENTS ALSO GNAW ON THE VARNISHED OR PAINTED WOOD OF BACKCOUNTRY SHELTERS, SIGNS AND OUTHOUSES:** Porcupines chew away at plywood to eat the glue. In addition, they enjoy the taste of rubber and can gnaw away at the hose lines and tires of vehicles.

• **TO AVOID HAVING VEHICLES VANDALIZED BY PUSHY PORCUPINES WHEN LEAVING VEHICLES AT A TRAILHEAD, RESOURCEFUL MOUNTAIN ADVENTURERS SURROUND THEM WITH CHICKEN WIRE:** This prevents the porcupines from feasting on the cooling hoses and other delectables.

RABIES

Rabies is a viral infection that causes infection of the brain (encephalitis) in people. It is usually fatal. Some people infected with rabies have survived although they have suffered severe brain damage as a result of the infection. Rabies can be transferred to humans by an infected animal. Almost all meat-eating animals are capable of transmitting this disease. However, rabies has largely been curbed in the United States and Canada by vaccinating domestic animals such as dogs. The incidence of rabies in domestic animals and people has declined dramatically in the last few decades.

The rabies virus is present in the saliva of an infected animal. It can be transmitted to a person by a bite from infected animals, or from the animal licking an open wound, or licking mucous membranes such as the lining of the mouth or eyelids. Bats, skunks, raccoons, groundhogs and foxes are the most common carriers of the rabies virus in wildlife. Strains of rabies associated with bats are the most common cause of the small number of human rabies cases in the United States. In some cases, only limited contact with the rabid bat took place. The virus can likely be passed to people if they breathe air contaminated by rabid animals such as bats.

How can you tell if a wild animal is rabid? Unusual behavior can indicate the presence of the disease. For example, animals that normally fear people can appear to be friendly instead of displaying signs of apprehension. Rabid bats can fly in midday. Some rabid animals such as skunks can even go after people instead of running away from them. An unprovoked attack by a wild animal can indicate rabies. Getting bitten by a wild animal while feeding it is not an unprovoked attack.

• IF A BAT SCRATCHES, BITES, OR PHYSICALLY CONTACTS YOU, OR A WILD ANIMAL BITES YOU, CONSIDER THAT THE ANIMAL COULD BE RABID AND TAKE ACTION TO MINIMIZE POSSIBLE INFECTION:

—IMMEDIATELY WASH THE SALIVA FROM THE WOUND: Use soap and water if available or even alcohol. Thorough washing can decrease the number of viruses that enter the wound.

—SEEK MEDICAL CARE AS SOON AS POSSIBLE: Medical practitioners could treat the wound by washing it with solutions that can kill some of the virus. If rabies is suspected, physicians might provide a vaccine to increase immunity to the disease as well as other treatments.

—REPORT THE INCIDENT TO YOUR LOCAL HEALTH DEPARTMENT: It will attempt to observe the suspect animal and determine whether it is rabid.

R A B I E S
(continued)

R I D G E S

RIDGES

A ridge can be composed of rock, ice or snow. The term generally describes the crest that is created when two faces of a mountain come together. Ridge can also be used to describe a pointed feature that stands apart from the main mountain such as a buttress. The French word *arête* (meaning fish-bone) describes a narrow ridge created by two glaciers eroding opposite sides of the same wall.

Many classic routes in the mountains follow ridges. This is partly because ridges lead to summits—the goal of many mountain adventurers. However, ridges offer other advantages. Routefinding is often fairly straightforward since the route simply follows the line of the ridge. Ridges also enable travelers to skirt above other terrain hazards such as cliffs, gullies and steep snow and scree slopes. Spurs of rock, buttresses and small ridges offer easier travel than a heavily forested valley or slope below.

Because ridge travel avoids hazards such as snowslopes, it also offers a certain freedom of timing. For example, descending a steep snowslope in the heat of the afternoon sun may be a poor choice if it is subject to avalanche danger. Being on the ridge, however, avoids the potential danger and does not pose such a severe time constraint.

A ridge can also have a gentler angle of ascent than a gully or system of cliff bands and ledges. If the weather is good, a ridge offers a far-ranging view of the surrounding environment as well as impending weather. On the other hand, ridges have their own set of hazards. They are exposed to wind, lightning and other weather. Unstable boulders and stacks of rocks can be found on the edges of cliffs. The crests can rise over steep terrain such as cliffs and gullies.

Be aware of the following safety factors when routefinding along ridges.

• WIND: Mountains and peaks act as a barrier to the flow of air. Air in the lower atmosphere, meeting the mountain barrier, is forced up crests and over peaks. As air rises, it cools. When the air descends the lee side, standing waves are created in the atmosphere.

The flow of the air follows the lay of the land. If the slope is quite gentle, the resulting wave of wind is also gentle. As the slope becomes more abrupt, a more pronounced wave of air is produced. When air flows down a sheer wall, steep waves are created. A turbulent mass of air can also be produced as the wind circles back towards the face.

"The rock was overlaid by a centimetre-thick film of ice and, whenever I broke through that crust with my crampons, the rubble went pounding down the Face by the hundred-weight."

—Heinrich Harrer

RIDGES
(continued)

Ridges often lead to summits—the goal of many mountain adventurers—but they also have positive and negative safety factors.

Local terrain features also produce certain wind patterns. Wind gathers speed when it is funneled through a gap in a ridge or a valley. This is known as the "Venturi Effect." Wind also increases in speed as it flows around the shoulder of a mountain. This is known as the "Island Effect."

Since the upper parts of ridges occur in the alpine zone where there are no trees, ridges do not offer any protection from wind. Sudden gusts of wind roaring over the top of a ridge could be strong enough to cause hikers to lose their balance. The flow of wind also produces a cooling effect by robbing the body of heat through convection (wind chill). As a result, people are often more prone to cold injuries such as hypothermia and frostbite on wind-blown ridges than in sheltered valleys.

• **WINDSPEED:** A gentle wind, blowing up to 11 MPH / 18 kph , lifts particles of snow only about 1 inch / 2.5 centimeters above the ground. A moderate wind, blowing 11 MPH / 18 kph miles per hour lifts snow about 1 foot / .3 meters above the ground. The particles begin to hop and bound with the force of the wind. A blizzard occurs when wind blows snow at 32 MPH / 50 kph or more. A strong wind, blowing at 22 MPH / 35 kph, can lift snow on the ground up to 330 feet / 100 meters in the air creating whiteout conditions.

• **TEMPERATURE:** Since air cools as it rises, a ridge is usually much colder than the valleys below. If the rising air cools below the freezing point, any water droplets in it will fall as snow. Snow is common on mountain ridges and peaks at any time of the year. The height at which snow remains year-round is referred to as the snowline. It varies according to latitude. As the Rocky Mountains advance northward, the snowline occurs at lower elevations.

Lingering snow can obscure the ridge and make it difficult to ascertain where the ridge proper ends. Cornices also occur on ridges and obscure the edge throughout the year at high elevations. Pockets of snow or rotten ice may also remain around outcrops of rock. Because of the relationship between tem-

"... it was no more than a guess of blue and remote white glimmer blending with the hem of the sky, but it spoke to them, out of memory and old tales, of the high and distant mountains."

—J.R.R. Tolkien

If this hiker had taken a ridge, he might have avoided this hazardous snowslope entirely.

perature and elevation, hikers and skiers can encounter snow at any time of the year on ridges, depending on the latitude.

Falling rain or snow also obscure visibility. As a result, mountain travelers could unknowingly proceed in a direction they would otherwise avoid. Ridges and summits are also targets for lightning strikes since they are the highest point in the surrounding terrain.

• **BOULDERS:** The combined forces of wind and weather blast off most of the smaller rocks along ridges. As a result, only large boulders or stacks of rock may remain. The boulders, subjected to weather, are usually eroded and unstable. Piles of loose rock can be precariously perched along the edge. This causes rockfall hazard. It may also cause the unwary hiker to twist an ankle or fall. See ROCKFALL.

"It's a round trip. Getting to the summit is optional, getting down is mandatory."

—Ed Viesturs

R I D G E S
(continued)

R O C K F A L L

A fairly straightforward ridge can also be broken by bands of rock or small cliffs. These pose challenges in routefinding and may require climbing skills. Sometimes, it may be necessary to traverse around the rock bands. This may present additional challenges in terrain and routefinding. The best option may also be to hike up and over the bands of rock. If a series of rock bands stand up along the ridge, going up and down them can be quite time-consuming.

• **EXPOSURE:** While some ridges are quite gentle, others are steep. A knife-edge ridge, for example, rises sharply on both sides, leaving the hiker only a narrow pointed crest to follow. Such a ridge has a precipitous drop off on both sides making the consequences of a fall very serious.

TIPS FOR SAFE TRAVELING ON RIDGES

• **CHECK THE WEATHER FORECAST:** If a storm is imminent, avoid ascending a ridge. Choose to hike or ski in a valley or more sheltered area instead. By making this choice, you will avoid the potential problems of lightning, severe winds, poor visibility and rockfall that characterize ridge travel.

• **KEEP AN EYE ON THE WEATHER AS YOU PROCEED UP THE RIDGE:** If a storm is threatening, or the wind becomes overpowering, descend. Seek temporary shelter behind a feature such as a large stable boulder. Consider marking your route if you are concerned about poor visibility.

• **TAKE YOUR LUNCH OR REST BREAK IN A SHELTERED AREA BEFORE REACHING THE CREST OF THE RIDGE:** This will provide protection from the cooling effect of the wind. In addition, in severe wind, put on a windproof layer before ascending the ridge. This keeps a layer of warm air next to your body and helps prevent you from cooling down too quickly.

• **KEEP WELL BACK FROM THE EDGE ESPECIALLY IF SNOW OBSCURES IT OR LOOSE BOULDERS OR STACKED ROCKS ARE PRESENT:** Before putting your weight on a large rock, take a look to see whether or not it is loose. If so, avoid it. This could prevent a potential slip or fall. It also stops rocks from falling on those below.

ROCKFALL

Rockfall can be a significant hazard in the mountains, especially in ranges such as Glacier National Park, Montana, where extensive erosion to the rock in this area has made it loose. In other areas of North America where granite prevails, the danger of rockfall is much less. The danger of rockfall is greatest where gravity accelerates the falling mass. The hazard is significant directly under the face of a cliff, since a dislodged rock will gain momentum as it falls. Rock gullies act as natural funnels and channel the rockfall downward. Rock can fall from either of the gully's walls, and rocks falling down from above bounce off the walls a few times before becoming channeled into the main passageway. At the toe of the gully, the opening can be relatively narrow, forcing a large amount of rockfall into a small space. Rockfall also occurs in snow gullies since it can ricochet off surrounding cliffs.

"Each fresh peak ascended teaches something."

—Sir Martin Conway

Rockfall hazard is significant directly under the face of a cliff, since a dislodged rock will gain momentum as it falls. Move quickly through areas like this.

WHAT INCREASES THE DANGER OF ROCKFALL?

ROCKFALL
(continued)

• **EROSION:** Cliffs are subjected to natural forces of erosion such as wind and water and so they are constantly being eroded. Scree slopes at the base of cliffs are formed by falling rock and will likely continue to grow over time. Softer rock is generally eroded more quickly than harder rock.

• **ASPECT AND STEEPNESS:** More rockfall occurs on steeper faces than on gradual slopes because of the natural pull of gravity. The direction the slope faces is a factor since certain slopes are subjected to greater weathering.

• **PEOPLE AND ANIMALS:** Animals and people dislodge rocks as they travel, sometimes dropping them on unwary travelers below.

R

ROCKFALL
(continued)

Rockfall is a hazard on scree slopes since hikers can kick rocks loose on people below them. Travel closely together or move one at a time on loose scree.

"For two days I slogged steadily up the valley of ice. The weather was good, the route obvious and without major obstacles. Because I was alone, however, even the mundane seemed charged with meaning."

—Jon Krakauer

• **LIGHTNING:** A lightning strike can jar rocks from unstable resting-places causing them to cascade down the slope. Weather can also generate rockfall. For example, high winds can displace rocks.

• **RAIN:** During a heavy rainstorm, water runs down steep faces, carrying rocks along with it.

• **MELTING SNOW:** When snow and ice melts in the spring, the running water moves rocks and loosens the masses of dirt and vegetation that hold piles of rocks together.

• **FREEZE/MELT CYCLE:** In the winter, water freezes in cracks in the rock. As it freezes, it expands, pushing the crack outwards. In the spring, when the ice melts, stones caught in cracks are released. Over time, cracks gradually get larger and the rock becomes weaker.

• **WEATHER:** When it is raining or warm temperatures melt snow, the resulting water runs down cracks in the rock and other natural funnels such as gullies. The force of the water loosens rock and other debris and carries it down the mountainside. Wind and lightning also produce rockfall.

• **TIME OF DAY:** As the rays of the sun reach the face of a high cliff, it melts ice holding small rocks and other debris. As a result, the danger of rockfall increases just after this occurs.

ROCKFALL
(continued)

TIPS FOR AVOIDING ROCKFALL

In general, the best way to avoid rockfall is to plan your route so you are not exposed to it, especially when weather or time of day increases the hazard. Consider the following precautions:

• **LOOK FOR SIGNS OF PAST ROCKFALL:** Check out the route before hand to find out if rockfall represents a hazard. Is a certain gully steep and narrow? Would it act like a funnel, channeling rockfall towards you? Look for indications of past rockfall such as piles of debris at the base of gullies or couloirs. Dark areas in snow may also indicate rockfall. If the danger of rockfall is high, change your route and/or take the precautionary measures described below.

—**TRAVEL CLOSELY TOGETHER OR MOVE ONE AT A TIME:** As you hike up a steep trail, rock gully, or snow couloir, you might kick rocks on people below you. The farther they are below you, the farther the rock has to travel, and the more momentum it will pick up.

—**TO REDUCE THE FORCE OF ROCKFALL, TRAVEL TOGETHER IN A GULLY OR COULOIR:** Have the person behind you travel immediately behind. Or, take different lines of travel, making sure you are not in the direct line of fall. Alternatively, if the rockfall hazard is high, move from safe place to safe place one at a time. Have one person move to a safe location, then have the next person move. If another party is ahead of you and the rockfall hazard is significant, wait until they clear the gully before starting up. If you dislodge a rock, try to stop it with your foot before it gathers momentum.

—**CROSS HAZARDOUS AREAS QUICKLY:** Do not stop in areas of high rockfall hazard. Instead, move quickly through the gully or couloir and stop only when you reach a safe area. If you must stop or travel below a cliff, try to find a place safe from rockfall.

—**WARN OTHERS IF YOU DISLODGE A ROCK:** If you kick a rock loose, immediately yell "Rock!" This call advises others to watch out for falling rock. The warning may give them sufficient time to get out of the way.

—**WEAR A HELMET IF DANGER OF ROCKFALL IS HIGH:** A helmet, especially one that meets North American climbing standards, helps protect the head from rockfall and other hazards.

—**AVOID RESTING IN AREAS SUBJECT TO ROCKFALL:** Find areas free from rockfall when you stop. Place your pack in a secure area where it will not be hit or dislodged by rockfall. If rockfall occurs, take cover in a protected area such as an overhang. Travel in stages in between volleys of rockfall.

ROUGH
TERRAIN

ROUGH TERRAIN

Terrain in the mountains is seldom flat or level, and at times it can be extremely challenging. When traveling in the high country scrutinize the terrain carefully to maximize the safety of routefinding in unfamiliar territory. Consider the following types of rough terrain and plan accordingly.

• **BROKEN GROUND:** It is easy to twist your ankle or wrench your knee on broken ground. Broken ground also occurs on steep terrain, which can cause you to slip down the slope. To minimize the hazards of traveling on broken ground, try these tips.

—INSTEAD OF HAPHAZARDLY SCRAMBLING OVER BROKEN GROUND, CHOOSE A ROUTE MAKING USE OF NATURAL BREAKS, LEDGES, OR ANIMAL TRAILS.

—IF YOU'RE GOING TO HIKE UP A STEEP SLOPE, MAKE SURE YOU ARE COMFORTABLE COMING BACK DOWN THE SAME WAY. OTHERWISE YOU CAN END UP STRANDED.

• **BOULDER FIELDS:** Boulder fields are characterized by an expanse of large, sturdy rocks. Negotiating a boulder field can be tricky because the boulders are usually variable in size and do not lie flat. It is easy to slip especially when the boulders are covered with snow, are wet, or are covered with vegetation. Travel slowly and carefully on boulder fields. Otherwise, you may slip and jam your foot in the rocks. This is especially hazardous if the boulder field is wet or snow-covered.

• **SCREE SLOPES:** Mountains, especially those formed of easily fractured rock, erode with the forces of wind and weather. Rocky debris falls and spreads out at the base of cliffs and gullies. A talus slope is gradually formed over time. Eventually, soil and vegetation begins to establish itself, filling up hollows at the base of rocks, and makes the slope more stable.

However, some slopes, especially younger ones, can be quite loose. Dislodging one rock can cause others to become loose and a small rockslide may result. Both small and large boulders, being precariously balanced, may wobble back and forth when pressure is placed upon them. When an entire slope is composed of small pieces of rock, it is called a scree slope.

Hiking up an unstable scree slope can be quite strenuous. Because the scree is not stable, your foot tends to slide backwards with every step. However, the characteristics that make scree difficult to ascend also make it enjoyable to descend. Descending a thousand feet or so of good scree can be accomplished in little time and with little effort.

However, scree slopes are also hazardous. Because your footing is not stable, it is easy to twist an ankle or stumble. Steep slabs can underlie loose scree making footing treacherous. Rockfall is a hazard on scree slopes because hikers can kick rocks loose on others below them. When descending a scree slope, it can be difficult to see if there are any rock bands or steps below. Although some steps can be small allowing you to negotiate them easily, others are steep cliff bands. You can find yourself caught on a cliff, uncomfortable going up or down. Consider these tips for traveling safely on scree covered slopes.

When traveling in the high country, carefully assess the terrain to find the best route through it.

—TAKE DELIBERATE STEPS INSTEAD OF SLIPPING AND SLIDING YOUR WAY UP OR DOWN THE SLOPE. IF YOU DISLODGE A ROCK, YELL "ROCK!" TO WARN OTHERS.

—SINCE ANOTHER HIKER MAY DISLODGE ROCKS AT YOU, AVOID STOPPING DIRECTLY UNDERNEATH THEM.

—TRAVEL IN A DIAGONAL LINE IF YOU'RE IN A GROUP. THIS WILL HELP PREVENT EITHER GETTING HIT BY ROCKFALL OR HITTING SOMEONE ELSE WITH IT.

—TO PROTECT YOUR HANDS SHOULD YOU FALL, WEAR A PAIR OF GLOVES. WEARING GAITERS WILL KEEP ROCKS FROM GETTING INSIDE YOUR BOOTS.

—IF YOUR FOOTING IS STABLE, YOU MIGHT BE ABLE TO DESCEND QUITE QUICKLY AND COMFORTABLY. HOWEVER, IF THE SCREE IS LARGE, VARIABLE OR COVERS SLABS, YOU MIGHT BE BETTER OFF DESCENDING SLOWLY.

ROUGH
TERRAIN
(continued)

SIGNALING FOR HELP

1. Let people know you need help. Alter the landscape so it no longer looks natural. Use whatever you have—color, contrast, movement—to make your signal look out of place. A red flare is a signal of distress. It is effective in dense forest.

2. Make a large "SOS" signal in an open area using rocks, logs, boughs or other available material. Each letter should be about 3 feet / 1 meter wide and about 18 feet / 5 meters high. This makes it visible to people flying above.

3. Be prepared. Always carry a pack containing emergency equipment such as a lighter, a mirror, or a flare. Wear bright-colored clothing to contrast with your surroundings. This helps searchers locate you more easily.

4. Use international distress signals correctly. Holding both arms up signals to others you need help. Three of anything at regular intervals signals distress: Three calls, three whistles, three smoke signals.

5. Make a hot fire, and create a lot of smoke. A hot fire is effective even under a thin cloud layer because the rising heat creates a "wave" in the layer.

6. Be clear about your intentions. Holding one arm up and one down signals you do not need help.

SNAKES

Rattlesnake

SNAKES

In North America, poisonous snakes include rattlesnakes, copperheads, cottonmouth or water moccasins, and coral snakes. If provoked, snakes can strike people and emit venom. The venom contains toxins, which can affect the blood, blood vessels, and nervous system, and can result in paralysis and death. However, only a very small percentage of snakebites are lethal.

Not all snakebites are the same. The composition and concentration of the venom varies depending on the species. For example, the venom of a copperhead is much weaker than that of a rattlesnake. Concentration of the venom also changes throughout the year. It is most potent in the spring when snakes emerge from hibernation. The size of the snake is also a factor. Larger snakes usually emit a larger amount of venom than smaller ones.

In addition, venom is not always injected when a poisonous snake strikes. It can deposit its venom on the surface of the skin, or its fangs might not pierce the skin. The strike can also be too superficial for venom to be injected.

AVOIDING SNAKE BITES

Generally, a snake only strikes if it feels threatened. This can occur if a person invades its space, or irritates it in some way. Take the following steps to avoid a close encounter with a snake:

• **MOST SNAKES STRIKE FAIRLY LOW TO THE GROUND:** When traveling in the mountains, wear rugged boots that cover the ankle. Most snakes do not strike above this level.

• **SINCE SNAKES ARE COLD-BLOODED, THEY CAN OFTEN BE FOUND SUNNING THEMSELVES ON ROCKS AND LOGS:** Before stepping over a log, or sitting on it, inspect it to see if a snake is present. Instead of your hand, use a stick to poke under logs or around stones where a snake might be lurking.

• **SNAKES ARE NOCTURNAL SO TAKE SPECIAL CARE AFTER DARK:** If you are in a place where gathering firewood is permitted, make sure to get it before night falls. When walking at night, use a flashlight to illuminate the path and surrounding area.

• **REFLEX STRIKES CAN OCCUR FOR SEVERAL HOURS AFTER A SNAKE DIES, AND ENVENOMATION IS POSSIBLE:** Avoid handling a snake even if you think it is dead.

MANAGING SNAKE BITES

If the victim can be transported to a medical facility in two hours or less, take action to limit the spread of venom and immobilize the bitten area.

• **DO NOT APPLY A TOURNIQUET, INCISE THE WOUND, OR ATTEMPT TO SUCK OUT THE VENOM:** Instead bandage the bitten area firmly and then immobilize it with a splint. Keep the bitten area at the same level as the victim's heart.

• **THE VICTIM SHOULD MOVE AS LITTLE AS POSSIBLE SINCE MOVEMENT SPEEDS BLOOD CIRCULATION:** This moves the venom away from the bite and spreads it throughout the body.

• **IF THE VICTIM CANNOT BE TAKEN TO A MEDICAL FACILITY IN ABOUT THREE HOURS, A PERSON WHO IS QUALIFIED IN THESE PROCEDURES MIGHT CONSIDER OTHER TREATMENT SUCH AS INCISION AND SUCTION:** See also ACCIDENT MANAGEMENT.

SNOW-COVERED
TERRAIN

SNOW-COVERED TERRAIN

Snow-covered terrain involves a number of factors ranging from avoiding dangerous cornices to managing the shifting conditions of summer snowfields. Different types of snow-covered terrain require different routefinding techniques.

CORNICES

A cornice is a wave-like deposit of snow that forms on the lee side of ridges or other features exposed to wind-drifted snow. Cornices are formed as a result of wind, terrain features, and snow. While cornices do not usually form on knife-edge or gentle ridges, they are often found on ridges having a moderate slope on one side and a steep cliff on the other.

The direction of the wind determines the location of a cornice. As wind flows up a ridge, it gains velocity and reaches its maximum speed at the top. In its upward travel, the wind picks up snow on the windward side of the ridge. When it descends the leeward side, the wind slows down and deposits the snow. If the ridge is steep enough, the speeding up and slowing down of the wind carves the snow deposits and eventually creates a cornice. As more snow is deposited, the cornice grows and begins to overhang the leeward side of the ridge.

Depending on factors such as storms, wind velocity, and the amount of snow, cornices can be soft and easily broken, or hard and solid. Although cornices usually form on the lee side of ridges, unusual or turbulent wind patterns can cause them to form on both sides of a ridge or even alternate.

A slab of soft snow, called a "snow cushion," can form below the cornice. Although the word "cushion" implies a small patch, a snow cushion may cover the entire leeward slope. Although cornices are most prevalent in winter, they can still be present in summer.

Traveling near or on top of a cornice is dangerous. If a person is on top of a cornice and it breaks, either from natural or human disturbance, it falls and he/she falls with it. There are also hazards associated with traveling below a cornice. If you are below it and it breaks, you may be hit by massive blocks of snow and other debris as it hurtles down the slope. The tremendous force of a falling cornice may also trigger an avalanche. However, through good routefinding, you can avoid most cornice hazards.

• **APPROACHING A CORNICE FROM THE WINDWARD SIDE:** Be aware of cornice hazard. When you approach the top of a ridge from the windward side, you can not be able to see if a cornice is present. From the windward side, a cornice can look like part of the ridge—a smooth slope extending out to the skyline. Since you do not know whether you are seeing a snow-covered ridge or a cornice, assume a cornice and take precautions.

—**DETERMINE PRESENCE OF A CORNICE:** Before you get too close to the top, stop and look at the terrain around you. If you discover that ridges, knolls and other features facing the same direction have cornices; the ridge you are on probably has one too. If you can, find a safe vantage point where you can see the leeward side of your ridge. Cornices can be present along the entire edge. If you have a ski pole, hiking stick or ice axe, probe the snow to see if there is rock underneath.

A cornice is a wave-like deposit of snow that forms on the lee side of ridges or other features exposed to wind-drifted snow. When traveling on a ridge, keep well away from the edge to avoid cornice hazard.

—**BE AWARE OF BUTTRESSES:** A series of buttresses can extend well out from the ridge. The snow-covered bays in between the buttresses can conceal huge cornices making it difficult to determine where the cornices end and the ridge begins.

—**LOOK FOR CRACKS OR INDENTATIONS:** Cracks in the snow can indicate a cornice has already partially collapsed. The crack is a fracture line—the point at which the cornice breaks.

—**STAY WELL BACK FROM THE FRACTURE LINE:** A cornice may fracture 30 feet / 10 meters or more back from its lip—the farthest extension of the cornice. As a cornice falls, it can take chunks of snow even beyond the fracture point along with it. If the ridge is entirely covered with snow, you may have difficulty estimating where a fracture can occur. How far to stay back is a point of debate since the safe area varies depending on cornice size and the nature of the terrain. As a result, your wisest choice could be to stay even farther back from the point at which you think you are safe.

—**AVOID GETTING TOO CLOSE TO THE EDGE:** If the snowy-looking ridge is actually a cornice, your risk increases with every step you take closer to the lip. Your weight could cause the cornice to break, and the lip will be the first to fall carrying you along with it.

• **APPROACHING A CORNICE FROM THE LEEWARD SIDE:** Be aware of cornice hazard. When traveling in terrain where cornices could form, stop and look up from time to time to see if cornices are present. If visibility is good, you can probably identify them by their characteristic wave-like appearance.

SNOW-COVERED
TERRAIN
(continued)

S

SNOW–COVERED
TERRAIN
(continued)

Snow can linger in the high country even in the summer months.

—**CONSIDER CORNICE STABILITY:** If it is very cold, cornices can be quite solid and thus fairly stable. They may slump and break down towards the end of winter, which increases stability. However, cornices can be quite unstable early in the season when they are forming, during a warm day or after a heavy snowfall.

—**ASSESS THE PATH OF THE CORNICE:** If a cornice broke, where would it travel? Will it plunge down a sheer rock face or a snow-covered slope? Could it trigger an avalanche?

—**AVOID TRAVELING UNDER THE CORNICE:** After establishing where the cornice could travel if it breaks, assess your route. Are you in its path? Keep away from the cornice's line of fall. Keep to trees or the tops of spurs. Determine your safest route and follow it.

—**FOLLOW AVALANCHE-TRAVEL PROCEDURES:** If you think a falling cornice could trigger an avalanche, take precautions when crossing the slope. Cross the hazardous area one at a time. See also AVALANCHES.

SUMMER SNOWFIELDS

A snowfield is more transitory than a glacier. It is formed when the winter snow melts in the spring and consolidates into large patches of snow. Some snowfields melt completely during the summer and form again the following winter. Others do not melt completely over the summer and remnants of them are present all year round. Over time, these snowfields may slowly melt, consolidate and become ice.

Traveling on a snowfield can be either quite enjoyable or extremely tiring depending on the conditions. If the snow is fairly well consolidated, you can walk across it fairly easily without sinking. It may be easier and faster, for example, to hike across a snowfield than cross a slope covered with boulders or other rocky terrain. However, conditions on snowfields are highly variable. Soft snow offers difficult traveling conditions. Sinking through to your knees as you cross a snowfield is extremely arduous. Traveling conditions on snowfields vary depending on a number of factors such as exposure, terrain, time of day, weather and season.

SNOW-COVERED
TERRAIN
(continued)

- **SLOPES FACING SOUTH AND WEST RECEIVE MORE SUN, WHICH CONSOLIDATES THEM AND THUS CAN BE FIRMER EARLIER IN THE SEASON THAN SLOPES FACING NORTH AND EAST.**

- **SNOW THAT IS DIRTY CAN BE FIRMER THAN "CLEAN" SNOW SINCE IT ABSORBS MORE HEAT. SNOW TENDS TO MELT OUT AROUND BOULDERS, TREES AND OTHER FEATURES, AND FORMS HOLLOW POCKETS IN THESE PLACES.**

- **SNOW EXPOSED TO THE AFTERNOON SUN MAY BE SOFTER THAN SNOW THAT IS SHELTERED BY SHADE, BOULDERS OR OTHER FEATURES.**

- **SNOW IS GENERALLY FIRMER IN THE MORNING THAN IN THE AFTERNOON WHEN IT IS WARMED BY THE SUN. HOWEVER, SNOWFIELDS CAN ALSO BE ICY AND HARDPACKED EARLY IN THE DAY. THIS PRODUCES SLICK FOOTING.**

- **SNOW CAN BE FAIRLY SOLID AFTER A COLD CLEAR NIGHT. HOWEVER, AN OVERNIGHT STORM MAY PRODUCE A DUSTING OF SNOW THAT HIDES TERRAIN FEATURES AND MAKES TRAVELING MORE HAZARDOUS.**

- **A SUMMER SNOWFIELD GENERALLY BECOMES MORE CONSOLIDATED THAN IN THE SPRING. AS SUMMER TURNS TO AUTUMN, HOWEVER, THE SNOW BECOMES HARDER AND MORE SLIPPERY.**

- **AS SNOW FALLING ON A SLOPE BEGINS TO SETTLE, IT "CREEPS" DOWNWARD. WHEN THE SNOW MOVES AWAY FROM FEATURES SUCH AS ROCKS, IT CREATES AN OPENING BETWEEN THE FEATURE AND THE SNOWBANK PROPER.**

Suncups are depressions in the snow formed when factors such as the movement of air and the presence of heat intensify irregularities in the surface. The hollows become deeply carved out, melting much more slowly than the points. They usually cover a whole snowfield rather than isolated patches. Large suncups can create tall columns of snow standing between the hollows. When they become pronounced, these pillars are called *nieve penitentes*, a Spanish word meaning "penitent snow." Traveling through deep suncups can be quite strenuous. But smaller suncups can serve as pleasant "stepping stones."

Hazardous terrain features also occur on snowfields. A moat forms near areas where a snowfield meets a cliff or other rocky feature. The radiant energy of the sun, warming the rock, causes the snow around it to melt. Moats can become quite deep. Falling in them could result in anything from wet feet to hypothermia or even drowning.

When it gets warmer, the snow melts and streams form. They vary in size from small hidden streams to fairly large channels. The result of slipping into a small stream could range from discomfort to falling in or being carried along in a large meltwater channel.

Snow also hides features such as logs and rocks. These features offer unstable footing or could give way. Over the course of the year, snow falls in depressions and other features, filling the terrain up with snow. The snow compacts and forms a bridge. The strength of the bridge depends on how well the snow has bonded.

In the spring, snow melts during the heat of the day and becomes weak. In

"I can't do with mountains at close quarters, they are always in the way, and they are so stupid, never moving and never doing anything but obtrude themselves."

—*D.H. Lawrence*

the evening, the snow freezes and becomes strong. Over the course of late spring and summer, the snow undergoes a series of these melt/freeze cycles. Over time, snowbridges begin to weaken and sag.

If the snow bridge is not strong, stepping on it can cause it to break. This may result in anything from a small fall to getting caught in the feature that lies below the snowbridge. Snowfields can release as they weaken in the afternoon sun. If the snowfield lies above a steep feature such as a cliff, the loosened snow can fall over the cliff, creating a type of avalanche.

TIPS FOR SAFE TRAVEL ON SNOWFIELDS

- **BEFORE CROSSING A SNOWFIELD, TAKE A MOMENT TO ASSESS THE QUALITY OF THE SNOW:** Does it offer good traveling conditions? If not, consider an alternate route.

    —**CONSIDER THE LOCATION OF THE SNOWFIELD. IS IT PERCHED ABOVE A STEEP GULLY OR CLIFF?** If you fell, or the snow avalanched, where would you end up? Choose a different route if the run-out is hazardous.

    —**CONSIDER FACTORS SUCH AS WEATHER AND TIME OF DAY WHEN DECIDING WHETHER TO CROSS A SNOWFIELD:** If it is overcast, the condition of the snow may not vary too much throughout the day. If it is hot, the snow may have a firm crust in the early morning and provide a good traveling surface (or it may be hardpacked and icy). By the late afternoon, however, under the full heat of the sun, the snowfield may turn into mush.

    —**IN SLUSHY CONDITIONS, SEEK SNOW THAT IS SHADOWED BY CLIFFS OR OTHER LARGE TERRAIN FEATURES:** It may offer a firmer traveling crust than snow exposed to the heat of the sun.

    —**SINCE SNOW MELTS OUT AROUND TERRAIN FEATURES SUCH AS LARGE ROCKS AND LOGS, AND FORMS HOLLOW POCKETS, AVOID TRAVELING TOO CLOSELY TO THEM:** If you step up on a log or rock, get off of it by taking a wide step.

    —**AVOID TRAVELING TOO CLOSELY TO MOATS. MOATS MAY FORM NEAR ROCK BANDS OR OTHER ROCK FEATURES.**

    —**USE A SKI POLE, ICE AXE, OR STICK TO PROBE THE SNOW IF YOU ARE IN DOUBT WHAT LIES BENEATH IT:** Do this when you suspect a snowbridge might collapse, or when you suspect a hazardous terrain feature such as a log.

    —**IF YOU SUSPECT A SMALL MELTWATER CHANNEL LIES BELOW THE SNOW, LOOK FOR DEPRESSIONS IN THE SNOW:** The color and texture of the snow might change if there is running water beneath it. Larger meltwater channels can lie underneath the surface and you may slide into them.

    —**THE EDGES OF A SNOWFIELD ARE OFTEN ICIER, SO BE ESPECIALLY CAREFUL WHEN MOVING ONTO OR OFF OF A FIELD.**

SUMMER SNOWSLOPES

Snowslopes vary in steepness. Some have a gentle angle while others are steep. Snowslopes offer a fast, enjoyable means of ascending or descending if snow conditions are good. A safe snowslope also offers a gentle run-out such as a valley. However, if the slope is steep and icy, it could result in a serious fall. If the slope ends at a hazardous run-out such as a cliff, the consequences of a fall could be even more severe. A snowslope can be subject to avalanche even in the summer. Cornices can also form at the top of snowslopes. Evaluating the safety of snowslopes is crucial.

"Nobody, however, had described the pitch when heavily iced over. The rock was absolutely glazed, offering no hold whatever to a frictioning foot."

—Heinrich Harrer

• **ASSESS THE STEEPNESS OF THE SLOPE:** A steep slope is usually more dangerous than a gentle one because you will probably gather speed more quickly if you fall. Slopes of 30 degrees and over—an angle that most downhill skiers enjoy—are generally considered steep. Assessing steepness can be problematic when looking directly down or up. For example, a concave slope gets steeper as you descend. To get the most accurate picture of steepness, you need to look at it from the side. If a slope looks steep, or you cannot determine its steepness, consider another route.

S

SNOW-COVERED
TERRAIN
(continued)

• **ASSESS WHERE YOU WOULD END UP IF YOU FELL:** If the slope has a hazardous run-out or if you can't see the run-out, avoid it. If you can't see the run-out, the slope might be concave in shape and steeper as you descend. Toss a rock or snowball. This may help to get a better idea of the steepness and runout.

• **ASSESS THE QUALITY OF THE SNOW:** Snow varies depending on many factors such as the season, the direction of the slope, the weather, and micro-environments such as a gully or clump of trees. Traveling on snow becomes more difficult when it becomes too slushy or too icy and hard. Avoid a snowslope if it does not offer safe or comfortable traveling conditions.

• **ASSESS EXISTING HAZARDS:** Since snowslopes may be subject to avalanche or cornice hazard, consider these before crossing the slope.

Snowblindness and Other Eye Disorders

Excessive exposure to ultraviolet radiation can cause eye fatigue. The eyes might also feel dry and gritty, as if sand has been rubbed into them. Over time, repeated exposure can result in the formation of cataracts. Too much ultraviolet radiation can also burn the surface of the eye, just as it burns the surface of the skin. Since snow reflects a significant amount of ultraviolet radiation, traveling on snow increases the amount reaching the eyes. Too much ultraviolet radiation can result in a condition known as snowblindness.

Similar to sunburn of the skin, snowblindness makes its presence known about eight hours after exposure. Sufferers may feel as though their eyes are irritated, are full of sand, or have an object in them. Any eye movement such as blinking can become very painful. Exposure to light can also be painful. The eyes may become red and start to tear. Although infrared radiation has not been shown to damage the eyes in normal dosage, it can cause them to feel dry.

• **TREATING SNOWBLINDNESS:**

– **Snowblindness heals naturally in a few days.** In the interim, however, it is important to avoid further exposure to the sun. If possible, rest in a dark environment. Avoid rubbing the eyes since this may irritate them further. Apply cool, wet compresses to the eyes. If the snowblindness is severe, patching the eyes prevents blinking and provides pain relief. If resting in a dark environment is not possible, shield the eyes from sunlight. Use sunglasses with side shields or goggles or both. Tape the lenses to prevent excessive light from leaking through.

• **PREVENTING SNOWBLINDNESS:**

–**Wear sunglasses that offer appropriate protection.** Check the label on the sunglasses to confirm whether they offer protection from ultraviolet and infrared radiation. Sunglasses are also available that offer special kinds of protection. Wear sunglasses even on cloudy days. Carry extra sunglasses or goggles in case of loss or breakage.

–**Use side shields.** This prevents reflected light from entering the sides of the eyes. Side shields also offer protection from infrared or heat rays. Makeshift side shields can be constructed from materials such as cardboard, cloth or tape. Removable shields are available at some mountain specialty stores.

S

SNOW-COVERED
TERRAIN
(continued)

TIPS FOR ASCENDING, DESCENDING AND TRAVERSING SNOWSLOPES

• **KICK STEPS WHEN ASCENDING.**

—Make short evenly spaced steps when ascending.

—This helps you maintain balance and provides good steps for others to follow. Kick the toe of your boot into the snow by swinging your leg. If you are in a group, take turns leading since kicking steps is strenuous.

• **MAKE SWITCHBACKS WHEN TRAVERSING.**

—Make steps by placing the entire foot in the snow.

—Traversing enables you to support your weight on your whole foot instead of just the toe. Switchbacking also enables you to alternate legs and thus reduce strain.

—Each person should kick firmly into the step so it does not become rounded and hazardous.

• **USE THE PLUNGE STEP WHEN DESCENDING.**

—Place your heel into the snow first.

—Since most of your weight will be on your descending foot, the snow (if soft enough) will slide forward slightly and then become compact enabling you to skid to a stop. Plunge stepping is easiest on a moderately angled slope with soft snow. It gets more difficult as the slope steepens and the snow hardens.

• **TAKE PRECAUTIONS WHEN GLISSADING.**

—Boot skiing or glissading can be done from either a standing or sitting position. Although it can be a fast and graceful means of descending, risk increases with speed.

—To decrease your speed in a standing glissade, crouch lower to the ground and spread your legs further apart. Keep one foot slightly ahead of the other so you can feel the upcoming terrain.

—To decrease your speed in a sitting glissade, sit fairly straight (instead of lying down) and place the heel of your boots on the surface on this snow. This enables you to use your heels as a brake.

• **USE SKI POLES OR AN ICE AX.**

—An ice axe is very helpful when crossing snow slopes. You can use it for balance, or to slow down or stop.

—Obtain instruction from a qualified mountaineering school on using ice axes and performing self-arrests.

—Alternatively, you can use ski poles to help arrest your speed when using plunge steps or a standing glissade. Take your wrist loops off to avoid wrenching your shoulders or arms if the pole gets stuck on a natural object or twists underneath you.

—You can also use a natural object such as a rock to decrease your speed or to stop when descending.

Take precautions when traveling in snow-covered terrain due to exposure to both direct and reflected ultraviolet radiation.

SOLAR RADIATION / SUNBURN

Solar radiation—energy from the sun—supports life on Earth. However, too much exposure to sunlight is harmful. In the mountains, solar radiation is a significant environmental hazard. In the entire spectrum of solar radiation, ultraviolet rays and infrared rays have the greatest potential for inflicting damage. Ultraviolet radiation has a shorter wavelength than visible light, while infrared has a longer wavelength. People experience infrared radiation as heat.

SOLAR
RADIATION
/
SUNBURN

There are three different types of ultraviolet radiation: UV-A, UV-B and UV-C. Of the three, UV-B has the potential to inflict the most damage. The atmosphere of the Earth filters out most of the UV-C radiation in sunlight. UV-A radiation is considered less damaging than UV-B.

In the mountains, the amount of harmful ultraviolet radiation that reaches adventurers depends on several environmental factors. At higher elevations, the atmosphere is thinner and screens out less sunlight than at lower elevations. Exposure to the direct rays of the sun is greater in the alpine than at lower elevations.

In addition, the icefields, glaciers and snowfields found in the alpine life zone reflect about 75% of the ultraviolet radiation. This exposes people to both reflected and direct ultraviolet radiation. Other environmental features such as water and wet grass also reflect radiation. The amount of radiation reflected may increase when in certain mountainous terrain such as bowls.

Exposure to ultraviolet radiation does not occur only on clear sunny days. Although features such as fog and clouds may partially shield direct sunlight, they tend to scatter much of the ultraviolet radiation throughout the sky. By receiving both direct and scattered ultraviolet radiation, a hiker may be exposed to more radiation on an overcast day than on a clear one. Time of day also effects the amount of solar radiation the Earth receives. The amount is greatest at the middle of the day when the sun is highest in the sky.

The amount of potentially damaging ultraviolet radiation the Earth receives is also related to the layer of ozone in the stratosphere. Ozone within this layer

S

absorbs ultraviolet radiation from the sun. However, scientific research over the last several decades indicates the amount of ozone in the stratosphere is decreasing. Among other concerns, this is producing "holes" of decreased ozone above Antarctica and recently above the northeastern parts of North America. This is a concern for hikers in places such as the Baffin Islands as well as in southern regions such as Patagonia and New Zealand.

SUNBURN

Sunburn results mainly from overexposure to UV-B. The increase of blood flow to the surface of the skin and the dilation of superficial blood vessels cause the skin to become red. Chemicals released from nerve endings cause sensations of pain and itching.

Burns range from mild to severe. A first-degree burn is usually red and painful with some swelling. A second-degree burn usually involves moderate pain and swelling with blistering, and a third degree burn damages the skin as well as underlying tissues.

Excessive exposure to sunlight causes degenerative changes in the skin and may result in skin cancer. People with light skin are at a greater risk of developing skin cancer than those with darker skin. Since the skin is part of the immune system, damaging it can lessen its ability to protect against infection. Sensitive parts of the body such as the face and neck are more susceptible to sunburn than other parts such as the limbs. Areas horizontal to the sun such as the shoulders receive more solar radiation than vertical areas such as the chest.

Some people are more sensitive to sunlight than others. Children become sunburned more easily than adults. (In addition, the effects of solar radiation are cumulative. As a result, it is more important for children to avoid excessive exposure to sunlight than adults.) Redheads and those with blond hair and blue eyes burn more easily than brunettes. Those who have more melanin in their skin are less susceptible to sunburn than those of northern European origin.

Some medications such as certain antibiotics increase sensitivity to sunlight. Coal tar and its derivatives also increase sensitivity. Some plants such as celery, limes, parsley and wild parsnip can cause topical photosensitivity if direct contact with the skin occurs.

PREVENTING SUNBURN

• **GRADUALLY INCREASE EXPOSURE:** Slow exposure to sunlight produces tanning and thickening of the skin. This helps protect the skin from sunburn.

• **USE AN EFFECTIVE SUNSCREEN:** Sunscreens containing para-aminobenzoic acid (PABA) filter out ultraviolet radiation that can harm the skin. However, they allow longer wavelengths that produce tanning to pass through.

Sunscreens are rated according to their sun protection factor (SPF). For example, a SPF of five enables the wearer to stay out in the sun five times longer than without sunscreen. SPF15 screens about 93% of ultraviolet radiation. Sunscreens with a higher SPF than 15 only provide marginally more protection. SPF 34 protects against 98% of ultraviolet radiation. Creams that block all ultraviolet radiation, such as zinc oxide, are also available.

• **APPLY SUNSCREEN PROPERLY:** Apply sunscreen liberally and pay special attention to areas that burn easily such as the face and neck, the tips of the ears, and the tip and bridge of the nose. Apply the sunscreen evenly and make sure the thickness is adequate. If possible, put in on about an hour or two before going out in the sun. This allows the sunscreen to penetrate the skin. Reapply the sunscreen throughout the day as needed. Most sunscreens indicate how long they are effective and if they have any special properties such as water resistance.

• **APPLY LIP PROTECTION:** Similar to the skin, the lips can also become sunburned. This may be followed by fever blisters or cold sores (Herpes simplex infections). To avoid this painful problem, liberally apply protective creams to the lips.

• **WEAR PROTECTIVE CLOTHING:** Clothing is a barrier and thus protects the skin from ultraviolet radiation. A broad-rimmed hat provides shade for both the face and eyes. Other hats shade the neck. Lightweight shirts and pants offer protection for arms and legs. However, thin clothing can let some ultraviolet through and does not provide complete protection.

• **PROTECT CHILDREN FROM ULTRAVIOLET RADIATION:** Reducing exposure to solar radiation during the first 18 years can significantly reduce the lifetime risk of skin cancer. Provide children with protective clothing; limit the time they spend in the sun or apply sunscreen with a SPF of 15 or higher. Since it is not advisable to apply sunscreen to babies who are six months old and under, limit their exposure to the sun and make sure they wear protective clothing.

TREATING SUNBURN

Sunburns are generally first-degree burns. However, very severe sunburn needs to be treated as a second-degree burn. For immediate first aid, place affected areas in cool water or apply cool compresses. This reduces swelling and prevents additional burning. If blisters are open, clean the area to prevent infection. If blisters are not open, avoid breaking them. Avoid putting lotions on blistered skin since infections can result. Avoid placing snow or ice on blisters since this may produce additional problems such as frostbite or hypothermia. In more severe cases of sunburn, dehydration may also be a issue.

SPIDERS (See also INSECT STINGS)

Spiders have fangs and produce toxic venom. However, most spiders do not pose a threat to people. Their fangs are not strong enough to pierce human skin or their venom is not strong enough to cause an adverse reaction. Illness-causing spiders are not present in the Canadian Rocky Mountains. However, the black widow, a spider capable of producing serious illness in people, is found in the United States.

TIPS FOR MANAGING SPIDER BITES

• **BLACK WIDOW:** A bite from a black widow spider can produce muscular cramps that start at the wound and then spread throughout the body. Among other symptoms, the patient can feel weak and experience tremors. The skin can be cold and clammy and the breathing labored. People bitten by a black widow spider can also experience nausea and dizziness. The symptoms worsen over a period of about a day and then gradually subside.

Black Widow

If bitten in the backcountry, do not attempt to incise the wound or suck out the venom. Do not apply anything to the site of the wound except for ice, which can relieve pain. If possible, capture the spider for later identification. Seek medical attention as soon as possible.

S

SPIDERS
(continued)

It is easy to slip on a steep snowslope. This mountaineer is increasing his safety by using a rope and an ice ax.

"I reached a huge scree-slope, of the kind one so often finds in the Julians, miles long. Down it I went, through the bleak hanging-valley, taking long bounding strides."

—Heinrich Harrer

• **BROWN SPIDER:** A bite from a brown spider can also produce illness in people. Following the bite, a blister forms at the site. The skin around the blister becomes inflamed and can become quite painful about eight hours after the bite. The blister bursts after about two weeks and the skin turns brown or black. The dead skin sloughs off in time. The pit that is left eventually heals although some scarring can occur. The patient can also experience symptoms such as pain in the joints, nausea and vomiting, and chills and fever. Fatalities have occurred but these are very rare.

If you suspect a brown spider has bitten you, try to capture it and bring it to a medical facility for identification. If it is identified as a brown spider, and you receive medical treatment in less than eight hours, physicians can cut out the site of the bite.

STEEP TERRAIN

Hikers and other mountain adventurers can unexpectedly come upon steep terrain for a variety of reasons. They can encounter challenges in judging the angle of a slope or meet with terrain difficulties such as slabs, ice or snow-covered rock, and loose rock.

One of the best ways to judge the angle of a slope is to look at it from the side. It is difficult to judge steepness when looking at it from directly above or below. For example, a convex slope becomes steeper as you descend; thus what looked like a gentle slope from the top may be quite abrupt in the middle or near the bottom. From the top, certain features may not be visible. Rock bands can be hidden from your view, while gentle grassy slopes may be apparent, giving you the impression a descent might only involve an easy hike down rolling terrain. Slabs of smooth rock may also not be immediately apparent as you look down the slope. Since slabs offer little in the way of holds, it is easy to slip when descending or ascending.

Steep grassy slopes can offer a good or a hazardous route depending on the conditions. If the grass is dry and the angle is not too steep, grass can offer a welcome change from either rock or snow. However, after a storm, long grass can be coated with a layer of water, ice or snow. This causes the grass to lie down similar to the grass on a thatched roof. Because of the slippery coating, it is difficult to dig your heels into the grass and get good footing. It is also easy to pick up speed on such a slope once a fall occurs. This results in no more than a quick ride down the grassy hill and a long laborious climb back up again. But if the grassy slope ends at a hazardous place such as a cliff, the consequences can be more serious.

TIPS FOR HANDLING STEEP TERRAIN

• **OBTAIN ACCURATE, UP-TO-DATE INFORMATION ABOUT YOUR INTENDED ROUTE AND REALISTICALLY APPRAISE WHETHER IT IS WITHIN YOUR ABILITIES:** Difficulty is in part a subjective assessment: What is easy for one person can be difficult for another. Build plans around the least able member of your party.

• **IF YOU ARE PLANNING TO TRAVEL ON STEEP TERRAIN, MAKE SURE YOU HAVE THE APPROPRIATE EQUIPMENT:** For example, running shoes do not provide adequate support in steep, slippery grassy terrain. Use sturdy hiking boots.

• **TAKE SMALL CHILDREN BY THE HAND WHEN TRAVELING ON STEEP TERRAIN:** Some hikers tether their children to themselves using a short piece of rope. This enables them to have two free hands and also be assured that their children are close by.

• **TAKE A LOOK AT THE SLOPE BEFORE CROSSING IT AND TRY TO PLAN A ROUTE:** For example, grassy slopes can have ledges or steps offering more stable ground than the slope itself. Animals could have made slight trails that could offer better traction than the slope itself. Avoid slippery places such as shaded areas that could be wet or covered by verglas. If you think the slope is dangerous—if it is wet and broken up by bands of rock or has a dangerous runout—consider another route.

S

STEEP
TERRAIN

"I don't want to overstate my rock climbing ability. I choose my routes pretty carefully. I always go with people who can catch me."

—Tom Brokaw

S

STEEP
TERRAIN
(continued)

When walking up steep terrain, place your entire foot on the ground instead of "tip-toeing" up the hill.

• **BEFORE TRAVELING ACROSS STEEP TERRAIN, CONSIDER WHAT WOULD HAPPEN IF YOU SLIPPED:** How far would you fall? Would you end up in a grassy valley or tumble over a cliff? Is the terrain stable or loose? Loose rock on a slab has a ballbearing effect. Can you see where you would end up if you fell? If you are not comfortable with your response to any of these questions, consider another route.

• **AVOID GOING TOO CLOSE TO THE EDGE:** There could be loose rock near the edge of a cliff that could cause you to slip. Or, in some instances, it is possible for the ground to give way, again causing you to fall. If you must venture near the edge, first secure yourself in some way such as by using a section of rope.

• **AVOID LETTING YOUR DESIRE TO ASCEND BLOCK YOUR BETTER JUDGEMENT:** Sometimes, in the zeal to reach an objective—whether it is the summit of a mountain, the top of a canyon, or a new valley—gets in the way of reason. Rationally, you might realize it would be better to stop, turn back, or try another route, but the excitement of the moment blurs these thoughts.

Follow the cardinal rule:

Do not climb up what you cannot climb down.

• **AVOID SHORTCUTS:** Making a good decision about whether an unknown route will "go" takes experience. If you are considering a shortcut, study the mountain at the start of your trip and along the way. As you ascend, look for possible descent routes. Evaluate the terrain to see whether a shortcut is viable. If in doubt, stay on the established trail.

WHEN HIKING TURNS TO CLIMBING

Accidents can occur when hikers unintentionally find themselves in steep terrain beyond their skill level. Since their intent is often just to go for a hike, they find themselves in a climber's terrain without a climber's protection. This can happen to skiers and other mountain adventurers as well as hikers. If you think a route looks good, only to find it is more difficult than you thought, return to more comfortable ground. Some people have a tendency to think the terrain will get easier once they skirt a difficult ledge or band of rock. This might not occur. The terrain could become more difficult too. Follow the cardinal rule: Do not climb up what you cannot climb down.

Use a walking stick for extra security on steep terrain.

If you have a guidebook describing scrambles or difficult hikes, bear in mind that difficulty is relative. What is easy for one person is difficult for another. In addition, if you get off route, you may find that the "easy scramble" is turning into something only mountaineers would enjoy. Follow one standard in the mountains: Your own. If you're not comfortable on the terrain, turn back, regardless of the route's designation.

TIPS FOR WALKING ON STEEP TERRAIN

• **AS THE ANGLE OF THE TERRAIN CHANGES, ADJUST YOUR WALKING STYLE TO DECREASE WEAR ON YOUR BODY AND INCREASE STABILITY:** Some people use one hiking pole while others find two provide greater security, especially when descending steep slopes.

• **WHEN WALKING UPHILL, PLACE YOUR ENTIRE FOOT ON THE GROUND RATHER THAN SCURRYING UPWARDS ON YOUR TOES:** Using the whole foot reduces muscular strain in your lower legs.

• **ON LOOSE SCREE, PLANT EACH FOOT FIRMLY AND BRIEFLY AND TEST ITS STABILITY BEFORE PUTTING YOUR WEIGHT ON IT.**

• **WHEN WALKING UP STEEP TERRAIN, PLACE YOUR FOOT SIDEWAYS TO THE SLOPE:** This edging technique also provides extra stability in soft surfaces such as soil or loose surfaces such as scree.

• **WHEN WALKING DOWNHILL, TAKE SHORT STEPS AND PLACE YOUR ENTIRE FOOT ON THE GROUND:** Use your hiking pole or walking stick for extra security. This also reduces strain on your knees. If you think you are about to slip, avoid leaning backwards as this will cause your feet to slip out from under you. Instead, keep upright or lean slightly forward.

Traveling on a ridge enables you to avoid the hazards that lie below it such as snow-covered terrain, loose rock, and slabs.

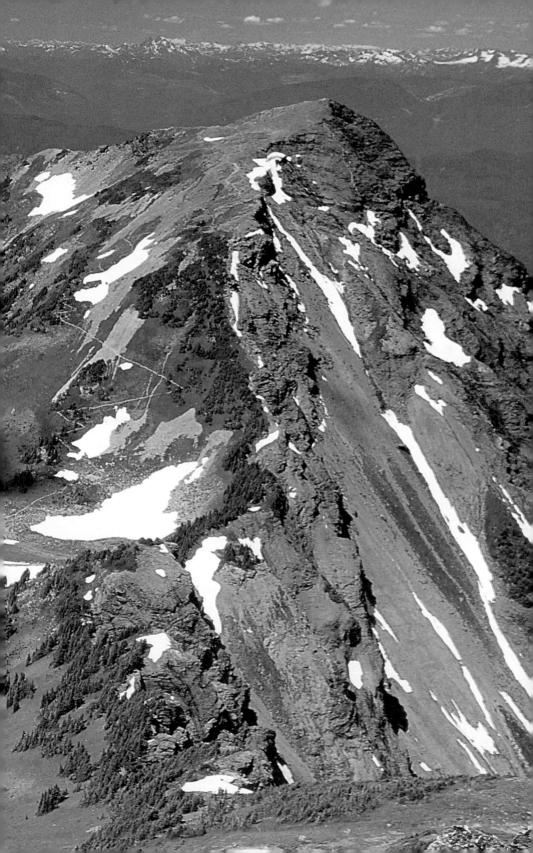

TICKS

TICKS

A tick is a blood-sucking parasite that attaches itself to four-legged animals such as dogs, and two-legged animals such as people. An adult tick looks like an insect but belongs to the Arachnid class, which includes spiders and mites. While an insect has three pairs of legs and a set of antennae, a tick has four sets of legs and no antennae. Different species are found in different regions of North America. They include the Rocky Mountain wood tick (*Dermacentor andersoni*), the American dog tick (*Dermacentor variabilis*), and the Lone star tick (*Amblyomma americanum*).

THE HAZARDS OF TICK BITES

Most tick bites on people are nothing more than an annoyance. You locate the tick and you extract it. End of story. However, ticks do carry certain diseases such as Rocky Mountain Spotted Fever, tick paralysis or Lyme disease as well as other extremely rare diseases.

Within two weeks of being bitten by a tick carrying Rocky Mountain Spotted Fever, an infected person can experience symptoms such as a sudden severe fever, muscle pain, and chills. Although antibiotics are effective against the disease, Rocky Mountain Spotted Fever can be fatal if untreated. Tick paralysis causes a loss of coordination and eventually paralysis in an infected person. However, recovery generally occurs within a few days of removal of the tick.

A few days to a few weeks after being bitten by a tick carrying Lyme disease, a distinctive rash called erythema migrans appears in about 75% of infected people. Often starting at the site of the bite, the rash looks like a bull's eye because it starts as a small red rash surrounded by a clear area. Flu-like symptoms such as headache, muscle aches, and fever can appear. If the disease is untreated, about 50% of infected people develop painful swollen joints and eventually can experience symptoms such as numbness, pain, fatigue, and depression. However, Lyme disease is generally not fatal.

TIPS FOR AVOIDING / MANAGING TICKS

- **ON THE TRAIL:**

    —**THE BEST WAY TO AVOID GETTING A TICK-TRANSMITTED DISEASE IS BY TAKING PRECAUTIONS IN TICK-INFESTED AREAS:** The greatest risk generally occurs from early spring, when the snow melts, to early summer when premature ticks are most prevalent. Avoid sitting or lying down in meadows where animals such as deer, elk and mountain sheep graze. Similarly, avoid rock bands and cliffs where bighorn sheep and mountain goats may have been present.

    —**INSTEAD OF SHORTS AND T-SHIRTS, WHICH LEAVE MUCH OF THE BODY EXPOSED, WEAR TROUSERS AND LONG-SLEEVED SHIRTS:** Tuck your pant legs into your socks and your shirt into your pants. Fasten your shirtsleeve tightly at your wrist. Wear a hat. If you have long hair, tuck it up under the hat. Wear shoes that cover your feet. These precautions help prevent the tick from getting under your clothing and crawling around where you cannot see it. In addition, wear light-colored clothing. This makes it easier to see any ticks that may have crawled up on you.

TICKS
(continued)

—AVOID BUSHWHACKING IN AREAS WHERE TICKS MAY BE PRESENT:
Stick to the middle of trails and try to avoid brushing against grass or shrubs. Ticks crawl up on low shrubbery and wait for large animals to walk by.

—CHECK YOURSELF FREQUENTLY FOR TICKS WHEN IN TICK-INFESTED AREAS: As soon as you see a tick on your clothing, brush it off, taking care not to touch it with your bare hands. If a tick has attached itself to you, extract it using the instructions in "Removing a Tick" below.

—SPRAYING CERTAIN INSECTICIDES (SUCH AS THOSE CONTAINING PER-METHRIN) ON CLOTHING AND SHOES MAY HELP DISSUADE TICKS FROM CRAWLING UP ON PEOPLE: However, some insecticides may have serious side effects. An insect repellent containing the ingredient DEET (N, N-diethyl-M-toluamide) can be sprayed on clothing or on the skin. But some people, children and infants in particular, may find high concentrations of DEET applied directly to the skin causes adverse reactions.

• **WHEN YOU GET HOME:**

—TICKS MAY BE PRESENT ON YOUR CLOTHING: Because of this, some people remove their hiking clothes before entering their home (and presumably put some other clothing on?). Others recommend giving clothing a thorough shake and inspection before bringing it inside your house.

—AFTER YOU PUT YOUR CLOTHES IN THE WASH, TAKE A HOT SHOWER AND INSPECT YOUR BODY THOR-OUGHLY FOR TICKS: Pay close attention to places where ticks are often found, such as the head and back of the neck, as well as warm hairy body parts such as the armpits and groin. Ask a friend to check your back or other parts you cannot see. Shampooing your hair does not remove ticks from it. If you have long hair, wash it several times and ask a friend to inspect it for ticks. Ticks often attach themselves to the back of the neck.

TICK

—CONTINUE TO CHECK FOR SEVERAL DAYS AFTER YOU GET HOME: Ticks can remain even after a person has had half a dozen hot showers.

—CHILDREN GET TICK-TRANSMITTED DISEASES MORE OFTEN THAN ADULTS DO, POSSIBLY BECAUSE THEY PLAY IN LOW-LYING GRASSES AND WOODED AREAS: Since children are often unaware of tick hazards, educate them about ticks, and have them follow the same precautions that you take.

TICKS
(continued)

TIPS FOR TICK REMOVAL

• **IF YOU FIND A TICK ON YOUR CLOTHING OR BODY, REMOVE IT AS SOON AS POSSIBLE:** Do not wait. Research on animals exposed to Ixodes ticks suggest they do not transmit infection until they have been attached for 48 hours. Since a similar time period may exist for people, removing a tick immediately will reduce the possibility of infection.

• **USE TWEEZERS OR WEAR RUBBER GLOVES OR PROTECT YOUR HANDS WITH CLOTH:** Although tick-transmitted diseases generally enter the bloodstream through the tick's saliva, Rocky Mountain Spotted Fever can be transmitted through contamination of the skin by tick blood or feces.

• **GRASP THE TICK AND PULL IT OUT STEADILY ENSURING YOU EXTRACT THE MOUTHPARTS:** Do not use your fingers. If you do, you will undoubtedly squeeze the tick and potentially inject tick saliva into the wound. Try not to squeeze or crush the tick since its bodily fluids may be infected and the bacteria may spill onto the skin.

• **FOLK REMEDIES RECOMMEND TOUCHING THE TICK WITH A LIGHTED CIGARETTE, A HOT NEEDLE, OR A FEW DROPS OF TURPENTINE OR AMMONIA:** However, it is better to avoid strategies like these. Stressed ticks are more likely to release bacteria through their mouthparts.

• **AFTER THE TICK IS REMOVED, APPLY AN ANTISEPTIC TO THE BITE:** Do not scratch it as the skin may become inflamed. Wash your hands thoroughly with soap and water. Flush the tick down the toilet. If it is put outside or in the garbage, it may revive and make its way back to you or another unsuspecting host.

• **SOME EXPERTS RECOMMEND THAT PEOPLE KEEP THE TICK AFTER EXTRACTION:** Place it in a sealed container such as a glass jar with a small amount of alcohol. Then, if the bitten person develops symptoms, he or she can ask a physician to examine the tick and determine if it was infected with a disease such as Rocky Mountain Spotted Fever or Lyme disease. See a doctor if:

—THE MOUTHPARTS OF THE TICK REMAIN EMBEDDED IN THE SKIN.

—THE SKIN BECOMES INFLAMED AFTER REMOVAL.

—YOU EXPERIENCE SEVERE HEADACHES, CONTINUOUS FEVER, OR A RASH WITHIN THREE DAYS TO TWO WEEKS OF A TICK BITE.

To make sure your pets do not get ticks, or pass them on to you, apply the same precautions for your pets that you do for yourself.

TICKPROOFING YOUR PET

Since dogs and other domestic animals such as cattle, horses, and cats pick up ticks, do not cuddle your pet if it has been exposed to a tick-infested area. It may pass the ticks on to you, or they may crawl off your pet and into the house. Certain tick-transmitted diseases, such as Lyme disease, are also found in domestic animals. Symptoms include fever, swollen glands and joints, and heart and nervous system problems. Changes in temperament have been noted in horses and dogs.

Left untreated, domestic animals may get arthritis. To make sure your pets do not get ticks, or pass them on to you, apply the same precautions for your pets that you do for yourself. Since most animals are lower to the ground than most adults, they are especially likely to pick up ticks if they run through grasslands, meadows, or rocky outcrops where large animals have been grazing.

T
TICKS
(continued)

• **ALTHOUGH TICKS CAN BE FOUND ANYWHERE ON A PET, CHECK THE HEAD, NECK, AND EARS IN PARTICULAR:** Ticks may also be found on the paws and in the groin.

• **FOLLOW THE PROCEDURES FOR TICK REMOVAL OUTLINED ABOVE:** Take care not to touch the tick with your bare hands and make sure its mouthparts are extracted.

• **ASK YOUR VETERINARIAN TO RECOMMEND A REPELLENT COLLAR, SUBSTANCE OR SOLUTION FOR YOUR PET:** A vaccination for Lyme disease is available for dogs and may be appropriate in areas where the disease occurs.

W A P I T I

Close encounters with wapiti are rare. However, if one occurs, do not lie down and play dead since ungulates strike out with their powerful front legs.

WAPITI (ELK)

Wapiti are the second largest member of the deer family, *Cervidae*, which is comprised of deer, moose, wapiti, and caribou. Males weigh about 700 pounds / 1540 kilograms while females weigh about 450 pounds / 990 kilograms. Distinguished by a white patch on their rump, wapiti are generally darker in color around the head and neck. "Wapiti" is a Shawnee name meaning, "white rump." The Europeans named these animals "elk." At one time, wapiti were found across the contiguous United States and in most Canadian provinces. Due to human encroachment, agriculture, and hunting, their numbers have declined although they continue to exist in mountain parks and other areas.

WAPITI AND PEOPLE

In the backcountry, wapiti do not generally pose a hazard to people since they are normally wary of them. In fact, seeing a majestic stag with a magnificent rack of antlers or a hine with a calf is an experience many people would cherish. However, wapiti that live close to people can present a different story. For example, in Banff National Park, Alberta, wapiti habitat has gradually shrunk because of roads and human development. As a result, more and more wapiti are attracted to the town by the ready availability of food in the form of lawns, succulent shrubbery, and lush flowers. The wapiti have a higher survival rate near the town where there is a greater absence of predators such as wolves. When the wapiti become habituated to people, they lose their natural wariness. People also get used to seeing wapiti in town and lose their fear of these large animals.

Wapiti Hoof Print

TIPS FOR AVOIDING ENCOUNTERS WITH HABITUATED WAPITI

• **STAY WELL AWAY FROM WAPITI—100 FEET / 30 METERS OR MORE:** These large animals are unpredictable and can charge.

• **AVOID SURPRISING THEM:** Make noise when hiking in an area where wapiti pose a hazard. Hike in a group and keep small children nearby. Be especially careful in areas of dense bush, near blind corners, and near rivers where the sound of water masks your presence. If out at night use a flashlight.

• **KEEP WELL AWAY FROM CALVING OR RUTTING AREAS:** Hines are more belligerent during the spring and stags are most hostile during the fall. During rutting season, stags are drawn into open areas where they can control the hines.

• **DON'T LET YOUR DOG RUN OFF LEASH:** Wapiti can strike out at dogs because they perceive them as predators (similar to coyotes and wolves).

• **OBEY POSTED SPEED LIMITS SINCE WAPITI OFTEN FEED NEAR ROADSIDES DURING THE SPRING AND FALL:** Slow down and do not overdrive your headlights. Wapiti could suddenly walk out on the road and cause serious damage to you and your vehicle.

• **REMAIN IN YOUR VEHICLE IF YOU STOP TO LOOK AT WAPITI:** These animals can charge if a person gets too close. The presence of a person can cause them to run out onto the highway into oncoming traffic.

TIPS FOR MANAGING ENCOUNTERS WITH HABITUATED WAPITI

If a person gets too close to a wapiti and it feels threatened, it could chase, attack, or run away. Wapiti can indicate nervousness by flicking their ears, looking toward you, their fur might bristle. The ears flicked back indicate aggression.

• **AVOID RUNNING:** A person cannot outrun a wapiti and attempting to do so may provoke it to chase you. Stand your ground.

• **IF POSSIBLE, BACK AWAY SLOWLY:** Find an area of greater safety such as behind a large tree or into a vehicle.

• **DO NOT PLAY DEAD IN A CLOSE ENCOUNTER WITH A WAPITI:** Ungulates can rear up and stomp down on a person with their front legs. Wapiti can also make bluff charges.

• **IF IT IS A HINE, TRY TO LOOK LARGER THAN YOU ARE:** Wave your arms over your head and talk in low tones. You might be able to convince the wapiti that you are bigger than it is.

• **IF IT IS A STAG, AVOID ACTING ASSERTIVELY:** The stag is easily recognizable in the fall by its antlers. It can interpret your assertiveness as a display of dominance and challenge you as a result. Avoid direct eye-to-eye contact, since it can interpret this as a provocation.

W A P I T I
(c o n t i n u e d)

Wapiti Antlers

Moose Antlers

Mule Deer
Antlers

WATER
HAZARDS

WATER HAZARDS

Water hazards can be one of the most challenging safety issues for people in the mountains. High country lakes and rivers not only obsure routes—posing significant routefinding puzzles— they also present numerous other water-related problems.

COLD WATER HYPOTHERMIA

Many mountain lakes are fed by snow and ice melt. They are cold at all times of the year. When you enter the water, the cold flowing water immediately carries your warm body heat away and puts you at risk for "immersion" hypothermia.

Unlike exposure hypothermia, which occurs gradually due to heat loss from evaporation, respiration or inadequate insulation, immersion hypothermia happens quickly. It is characterized by the rapid loss of heat through conduction to cold water. The body loses heat about 25 times faster in cold water than in cold air. Some studies suggest about 50% of drowning victims do not die from water filling their lungs; instead, hypothermia is the cause. Sudden immersion in cold water causes quick heat loss from your skin and outer tissues. After about 15 minutes of immersion in cold water, heat is lost from the major internal organs. This causes your core temperature to drop. Your arms and legs become numb and you could lose consciousness and then drown.

The rate at which the body cools depends on several factors such as the temperature of the water, the percentage of body fat and the amount of protective clothing worn. Water does not have to be snow or ice-covered to produce immersion hypothermia.

TIPS FOR SURVIVING IMMERSION IN COLD WATER

The most important strategy for surviving immersion in cold water is minimizing the amount of heat you lose. This can be accomplished in the following ways.

- **IF YOU ARE WEARING CLOTHES, KEEP THEM ON:** If you are wearing a jacket, zip it up. If you have a hat, put it on. Your body heat will slightly warm the water between your body and your clothes and this slows heat loss.

- **TRY TO GET AS MUCH OF YOUR BODY OUT OF THE WATER AS YOU CAN:** Climb or lean out onto a log, part of a boat or any other floating object. Do this as soon as you can—before your hands and legs get numb.

- **REMAIN STILL INSTEAD OF SWIMMING ABOUT UNLESS YOU CAN REACH A NEARBY BOAT OR OTHER FLOATING OBJECT:** Attempt to keep calm and conserve your energy. When you swim, the warm water trapped between your body and your clothing is pumped and replaced by cold air. This chills your body. In addition, swimming or flailing about pumps warm blood to your extremities. This takes warmth away from your core and reduces your survival time by about 50%.

- **IF YOU ARE UNABLE TO GET OUT OF THE WATER, TRY NOT TO PANIC:** Attempt to conserve heat by using the Heat Escape Lessening Position (HELP).

  —HOLD YOUR KNEES TO YOUR CHEST. THIS PROTECTS YOUR TRUNK FROM HEAT LOSS.

  —WRAP YOUR ARMS AROUND YOUR LEGS AND CLASP YOUR HANDS TOGETHER.

  —IF THERE ARE TWO OR THREE OF YOU, HUDDLE TOGETHER. DOING THIS PROLONGS YOUR SURVIVAL TIME ABOUT 50% OVER TREADING WATER OR SWIMMING.

"And amid all this varied throng of sounds I heard the smothered bumping and rumbling of boulders on the bottom as they were shoving and rolling forward against one another in a wild rush, after having lain still for probably 100 years or more."

—John Muir

WATER CROSSINGS

Crossing swollen mountain rivers and creeks can be extremely hazardous because the danger of falling in and drowning is always present. Injuries also result from being swept up against obstacles such as trees and rocks.

Other hazards include immersion hypothermia. At the same temperature, water conducts heat away from a warm body about twenty-five times faster than air. After 20 minutes of immersion in water at a temperature of 39°F / 12°C a fully clothed adult will lose consciousness. About half an hour later, that person will be dead. In some mountainous areas, water hazards account for more injuries and deaths than all other terrain features combined.

Loss of equipment is also a concern. In fast flowing water, backpacks and other equipment can be swept away. These include the mountain adventurer's survival gear such as tents, sleeping bags, extra clothing, stoves, and food. The loss of these important items could change a pleasurable overnight outing into a tragic epic. Problems also result when equipment is not lost but gets soaking wet. For example, some sleeping bags lose their insulating properties when wet.

Learning how to read a river and find a safe route is complex and beyond the scope of this book. However, a few pointers are provided primarily to help hikers identify safe crossing points. Research major river crossings before you start as part of your trip planning. Talk to knowledgeable people such as park rangers and get information on current conditions such as water levels, bridge washouts, and amount of snow. Knowledgeable people can offer advice on the best places to cross or even suggest alternate routes.

Water levels are usually highest after a heavy thunderstorm or when snowmelt is at its peak. The water level also changes throughout the day and the seasons. It is usually lowest in the early morning before the sun melts snow and causes the water to rise. Water levels swell in the summer when mountain snowmelt is at its peak and are at the lowest point in the fall.

Once on your trip, however, make sure you study the river carefully before attempting to cross. Observe the river carefully and consider aspects such as depth when deciding upon the safest place to cross. The run-out is also important; this is where you would end up if you fell. Remember that crossing water is very strenuous: water is about 80 times thicker than air so it takes much more energy to travel through it. Ask yourself: Can this crossing be avoided?

RIVER HAZARDS

Partially submerged boulders, sweepers (trees that hang down from the banks into the water) and logjams can be present in the river. Keep well away from sweepers because there could be additional logs hidden underneath the surface of the water. Logjams can offer a temporary footbridge if they are stable. However, it is also possible to slip and become jammed between logs.

The riverbed is also a consideration in crossing rivers safely. A level riverbed composed of gravel is an ideal crossing surface. However, some riverbeds are composed of a mixture of large and small boulders, which make footing difficult. You may be able to get some indication of the presence of boulders by listening for the sound of boulders banging and grinding in the current.

In hazardous river beds, your feet could become entrapped between boulders or in bedrock. Rocks that are polished by water can be smooth and offer little traction. Similarly, rocks and logs can be covered with slippery algae or weeds.

WATER
HAZARDS
(continued)

**W A T E R
H A Z A R D S**
(c o n t i n u e d)

Carry an extra pair of rubber booties, lightweight runners or sandals for river crossings. Rubber booties have the advantage of keeping your feet warm. Runners protect the feet but take time to dry afterwards. Sandals are light and dry off quickly but do not completely protect the foot from hazards such as sharp rocks. In any event, having an extra pair of shoes will enable you to keep your hiking boots dry. Some people find they are less likely to rush the river crossing when they have an extra pair of shoes. The added degree of comfort gives them the confidence to cross the river carefully and cautiously.

If you do not have extra boots, carry an extra pair of socks and put the dry socks on after you cross. Or, take your socks off, wear your boots to cross, and then put your socks back on after you have crossed.

Consider where you would end up if you were swept under. Does the river tumble over a cliff or other hazardous terrain feature? If so, do not cross. Consider how easily you can get out of the water once you have crossed the river. Are there steep banks or rock bands on the other side? If so, find a safer route.

TIPS FOR ASSESSING A WATER CROSSING

• **DEPTH:** Before crossing a mountain river or stream, assess the hazards. The depth of the water is of serious concern. It is easy to underestimate the depth of the river from the shore. It can be shallow near the banks and much deeper in the middle of the river. The depth may also be variable, as there could be deep holes in the river. Heavy rain will also cause the water level to rise. If the river is downstream from a dam, it may rise quickly and unexpectedly if the flow is increased.

—**WATER THAT IS GREATER THAN ONE FOOT / 30 CENTIMETERS DEEP DEMANDS SERIOUS CONSIDERATION:** Water knee-deep or over is very dangerous. If the water level is too high, do not cross. Wait until the level goes down, find an alternate route, or turn back.

—**CROSS AT THE WIDEST POINT:** If you choose to cross, consider crossing the river at its widest point because it will usually be shallowest there.

—**CROSS SMALL STREAMS VERSUS WIDE CHANNELS:** If the river has a series of braided streams, cross many of the small streams rather than the largest channel.

—**ROCKS AND LOGS OFFER A NATURAL FOOTBRIDGE:** It can also be possible to make a temporary bridge from logs and other deadfall. This can be stabilized using large rocks.

—**UNDO BOTH THE HIP AND CHEST BELT ON YOUR BACKPACK BEFORE YOU CROSS:** If you fall in, your backpack will fill with water and become very heavy and pull you underwater. By undoing the belts before you cross, you can quickly get rid of the pack before it drags you down.

• **SPEED:** Also consider the flow or speed of the river. Never underestimate the power of moving water: It exerts a tremendous hydraulic force upon objects in its path. The force of the water could also push you into obstructions such as rocks and other debris. The stronger the current, the more powerful the force. A strong current will sweep you off your feet and into the water.

When the dam burst, slabs of blue ice tumbled down the swollen river, surfacing and diving like sapphire dolphins.

*—Thomas
Wharton*

RIVER CROSSING

1. Water flows faster on the outside of river bends. Riverbanks can be steep making ascension difficult. Undertows may be present due to whirling currents. Avoid bends in the river.

2. If you slip while crossing water, keep your feet—not your head—downstream. Use your legs to push off from obstructions. Use your arms to help you push off if required.

3. The slope of the riverbed affects the flow of water. A fairly flat angle followed by a steeper angle followed by a flat angle creates turbulence. This increases as the angle increases. Avoid changes in slope. When water flows over, but does not completely cover, an obstruction such as a boulder, it may create a "pillow" of water on the upstream side. Avoid obstructions.

4. Many factors such as slope, depth, and the width of the channel affect how water flows. Water usually flows through a wide channel more slowly than through a narrow one. Favor slow-moving water. Before you cross, assess where you want to end up. Choose a flat area to complete your crossing. It is easier to jump from a stepping stone to even terrain than climb a steep bank.

5. Use natural features such as small boulders as stepping stones to make a bridge. Hop from stone to stone across the river. Take your socks off and wear your boots across. Put your dry socks on after you cross. Or, wear sandals or neoprene booties when crossing to make sure your hiking boots do not get wet. Make sure the belt of your pack is not clipped around your waist. If you

fell, the extra weight of the pack could pull you down and make navigation difficult. Alternatively, throw your pack across the stream and cross without your pack. Use a long stick or a ski pole when crossing. This "third leg," held in the upstream hand, provides extra stability. Face slightly upstream when crossing to avoid buckling of your knees by the flowing water.

6. The river can change throughout the day. It can be slow and shallow in the early morning or sunset. It can peak in the mid-afternoon as the sun melts snow. The flow can change due to human activities such as dams. Choose the best time of day for crossing.

W

WATER
HAZARDS
(continued)

—AVOID CROSSING AT PLACES WHERE THE CURRENT IS STRONG SUCH AS BENDS IN THE RIVER: There is a potential for undertows at river bends and steep banks can also be present. The current will also be strongest at narrow gaps in the river where the water is funneled. Instead, seek the point where the current is the slowest (usually the widest point in the river).

—IF YOU BECOME CAUGHT IN A CURRENT, DO NOT ATTEMPT TO STRUGGLE AGAINST IT: Continue to cross moving diagonally with the current across the river.

—IF YOU ARE CARRYING A MOUNTAIN BIKE, PLACE IT ON YOUR DOWNSTREAM SIDE: Otherwise the force of the current could push the bike onto you and trap you underneath it. Wear a helmet to prevent a possible head injury.

—LOOK FOR A WAY TO MAINTAIN BALANCE: Using a pole or linking arms with a buddy can help you keep your balance while crossing.

WATER CROSSING TECHNIQUES

If you are crossing alone, use a pole or stick for support. You can also use the pole to probe for depressions or obstructions in the riverbed as you cross. Make sure the pole is upstream rather than downstream. Facing upstream will also help prevent your knees from buckling. As you step across the current, lean against the pole for support. Move one foot at a time and rotate your hips with the current.

If there are two or three of you, it is safer to cross in a group rather than alone because each person helps support the others. One way to do this is by crossing in a line. Put the weakest person in the middle and link arms tightly. Move parallel to the current and continue to keep arms linked together tightly until everyone is safely across.

Three people can also cross together in a huddle. In this configuration, people bend forwards slightly at the waist and link their arms over each other's shoulders. The strongest person should be upstream and enter the water first. The huddle formation is quite stable, especially in fast, shallow water.

Cold Water Survival Times

The chart below indicates survival times for the average adult; however, this varies according from person to person. For example, people who are thin lose body heat more quickly than those who are heavy and children usually lose heat more quickly than adults. Other factors include the temperature of the air and water, water currents, wind and waves.

Water Temperature	Expected time before exhaustion or unconsciousness	Expected time of survival
32.5 F / 2C	Under 15 minutes	45 minutes
32.5F / 2C to 40F / 4C	15 to 30 minutes	30 to 90 minutes
40F / 4C to 50F / 10C	30 to 60 minutes	1 to 3 hours
50F / 10C to 60F / 15C	1 to 2 hours	1 to 6 hours
60F / 15C to 70F / 21C	2 to 7 hours	2 to 40 hours
70F / 21C to 80F / 26C	3 to 12 hours	3 hours to indefinite
Over 80F / 26C	Indefinite	Indefinite

Carry objects downstream of your body when crossing rivers and streams.

FROZEN BODIES OF WATER

Crossing frozen streams and lakes is dangerous because the ice could break and you could fall in. The result may vary from getting chilled and uncomfortable to severe cold injuries or death from cold water immersion. Experts say that at least 6 inches / 15 centimeters of ice is required to safely walk on it. At least 10 inches / 25 centimeters is required for small vehicles such as snowmobiles, and at least 12 inches / 30 centimeters is needed for vehicles.

Assessing the thickness of the ice is not always straightforward. For example, a thick blanket of snow can obscure the ice making it difficult to judge thickness. The ice can also be frozen more solidly in some areas than others. Still and shallow water freezes more quickly than deep and flowing water. The time of day also changes the strength of the ice. A body of water that is frozen sufficiently in the morning could weaken by the afternoon if warmed by the sun.

Obstructions within and around the body of the water also play a role in ice formation. For example, weak patches of ice can surround large boulders, heated by the sun. A spring can cause water to flow upwards and melt out the ice above and around it. The places where water enters or exits a lake or stream will likely be weaker than other areas because of the flow of water.

TIPS FOR CROSSING FROZEN BODIES OF WATER

• BEFORE YOU CROSS:

—RELEASE YOUR HIP BELT AND CHEST STRAPS BEFORE CROSSING: This enables you to get rid of your pack quickly should you fall through.

"What worries me right now are the melt streams up there. ... If somebody fell into one he'd be gone, whoosh, and down a mill hole quicker than a rabbit."

—Thomas Wharton

WATER
HAZARDS
(continued)

WILDFIRES

—**DISTRIBUTE YOUR WEIGHT USING SKIS OR SNOWSHOES RATHER THAN AT-TEMPTING TO WALK ACROSS:** If they become iced up, take them off when you reach the shore not while crossing. If you are in a group, spread apart rather than travel closely together.

—**USE A SKI POLE OR STICK TO CONSTANTLY TEST THE ICE AS YOU TRAVEL:** Thin ice and solid ice make different sounds. If thin ice has formed over an air pocket, you may hear a hollow sound when you test it. If your pole breaks through the ice, turn back and find an alternate route. If you suspect a section of ice is weak, move away to a safer location. Brush away the snow and chip out a small area of ice to assess its strength.

• **IF YOU FALL IN:**

—**IF THE ICE BREAKS AND YOU FALL IN, ATTEMPT TO GET OUT BY PRESSING YOUR ARMS OUTWARD OVER THE ICE AND BY MAKING YOUR BODY LEVEL:** Even if the ice breaks, continue to try to pull yourself onto the ice. Once on the ice, stay flat to distribute your weight. Crawl or roll towards shore rather than standing up.

• **IF YOUR FRIEND FALLS IN:**

—**WHEN HELPING OTHERS, AVOID GETTING TOO CLOSE TO THE HOLE YOURSELF:** Instead of walking up to the hole, spread your weight evenly across the ice by crawling up to the hole.

—**AVOID EXTENDING YOUR ARM OR LEG SINCE THE PERSON MIGHT PANIC AND PULL YOU IN:** Provide a ski pole, stick or rope instead. Place extra skis or branches around the hole to help distribute weight as the person gets out.

—**AS SOON AS POSSIBLE, GET OFF THE ICE AND TO A SAFE PLACE:** Immediately treat the person for hypothermia.

WILDFIRES

A wildfire is a natural part of the mountain environment and there are three major types: surface, ground, and crown. A surface fire, the most common wildfire, slowly burns along the forest floor. A ground fire, which is often started by lightning, burns either along or below the forest floor. A crown fire, as the name suggests, burns along the top of the forest. For both people and animals, getting trapped in a wildfire is a life-threatening situation. People can burn from the intense heat radiated by the fire, or suffocate from inhaling the dense smoke. People who enjoy mountain activities such as birdwatching, cycling, hiking, and camping are at risk when the fire hazard is high.

AVOIDING BEING TRAPPED IN A WILDFIRE

Before venturing into the backcountry, find what the fire hazard is in the area that you plan to visit. If it is high, avoiding the area is the most prudent decision. If you decide to visit the mountains when wildfires are possible, carefully plan your route before you go. Avoid places that are particularly hazardous such as dense brush, thickly wooded areas, and narrow canyons. Seek routes where the fire hazard is less such as sparsely vegetated areas. Identify safety zones along your route such as large bodies of water. Identify escape routes should a wildfire occur. These include areas where the lack of combustible material or the terrain enables you to escape from the path of a wildfire. As you travel in the mountains, be alert for conditions that could increase the fire hazard such as high temperatures or drought. Watch out for signs of wildfire. This includes smoke, which may permeate a large area around the fire. Be aware of the presence, speed, and direction of wind as it can greatly increase the fire hazard. If you become aware of a wildfire, do not panic. Take a few moments to evaluate your situation. Where is the fire located? What is its most probable path? If you can, get out of the probable path of the wildfire. Work your way toward the back of the fire. It is least hot at the back and most hot at the front.

WILDFIRES
(continued)

INCREASING THE SAFETY MARGIN IF TRAPPED IN A WILDFIRE

If you cannot escape from the path of the wildfire, do not try to fight it or outrun it. Instead, consider whether you could cross through the fire, or find terrain that offers shelter. In addition, try to protect yourself from the fire by wearing clothing such as trousers instead of shorts. Try to cover exposed skin with whatever clothing or material is available. (Please note that some materials, such as synthetics, are more flammable than others, such as wool.

• **CROSSING A FIRE:** Some experts recommend crossing the fire only if the flames are low and the area burning is quite small. If the flames are higher than your waist, or cover an area greater than three meters wide, do not attempt to cross the fire. If you do attempt to cross the fire, first determine your objective. You should aim for terrain that has already burned, or places that will not burn such as a large pond. Watch the fire and locate a place where it is burning quietly. Look for the easiest path through the fire—a path that offers good footing and does not have significant obstructions such as heavy deadfall, or dips and rises in the ground. Wait until there is a lull in the fire. Take several deep breaths before you go, and then try to move quickly through the fire to your objective using the easiest path.

•**SEEKING SHELTER WITHIN A FIRE:** If you do not attempt to cross the fire, look for terrain that offers protection from it. If you can reach a nearby water source such as a lake, pond, river, or creek, go to it and crouch in it. Cover your head, neck, and other exposed parts with wet clothing. Place some wet clothing such as a T-shirt in front of your face and breathe through it. Stay in the water until the fire passes. When you return to burned areas, exercise caution because hot spots can flare up suddenly. If you cannot find a nearby water source, look for terrain that is less combustible. These include places such as rocky streambeds, clear or sparsely vegetated areas, and rocky terrain. Try to find terrain that is large enough to put considerable room between you and the fire. If you can, remove combustible material in the immediately vicinity of your chosen spot. Try to find terrain within your spot that also provides a barricade between you and the fire. This could include obstacles such as a large rock or terrain such as a ditch. When you have selected the place that offers the best protection, lie flat in it. Try to cover yourself as well as you can with whatever material you have. In addition to clothing, soil can be used as a cover. To protect yourself from the smoke, try to breathe the air close to the ground. It will be cooler than the air above.

• **CREATING SHELTER WITHIN A FIRE:** If you cannot escape from the path of the fire, and cannot find suitable shelter near by, you could try to create an area of greater safety around you by decreasing the combustible material around you. First look for an area that is less combustible than other places such as sparsely vegetated terrain. With your back to the approaching wildfire and the wind, set the area on fire. Wait until a suitable large area has burned, and then move onto the burned terrain. Try to find an obstacle such as a rock to provide a barrier between you and the fire.

Despite images of wolves conjured in stories such as Little Red Riding Hood, *wolves are solitary animals and avoid people.*

W O L V E S

WOLVES

The gray wolf (*Canis lupus*), commonly called timber wolf, is the largest member of the dog family (*Canidae*). It varies in color and can be gray, black, white, or brown. The wolf has characteristic yellow eyes. The gray wolf weighs about 110-130 pounds / 50-60 kilograms. The females are slightly smaller than the males. Wolves are larger than coyotes and their tails are shorter. A wolf holds its tail straight when running, while a coyote allows its tail to droop. A wolf has a longer stride (about 62 inches / 158 centimeters when trotting) than a coyote and a larger print.

Wolves live in packs and have a highly defined social structure. The leader is called the alpha male and his partner, the alpha female. Generally mating for life, they are often the only breeding pair in the group. Wolves regulate their populations: When their numbers exceed available food, their fertility drops. The number of wolves in a pack varies from two to thirty and averages between five and twelve. Wolves are found in various habitats but favor forested terrain or the edge of forest and meadows.

Wolf packs avoid each other and maintain their own territories. They howl to identify their territories, reassemble their pack, and possibly to enjoy themselves. Depending on their prey, and its migratory patterns, the territory of a wolf pack may range from about 20 to over 700 square miles / 52 to over 1,815 square kilometers. Wolves are carnivorous and prey on animals such as mule deer, elk, moose, and bighorn sheep.

"I cannot say whether them {wolves} or the Buffalo are most numerous."

—Anthony Henday; diary entry 1754

PEOPLE AND WOLVES

According to fairy tales such as *Little Red Riding Hood*, people should fear wolves. But this is a myth rather than a reality. Wolves do not prey on people. Encounters between people and wolves are rare and seldom result in injury. However, some researchers believe anecdotal stories that indicate native peoples such as the Canadian Inuit may have been attacked in the wilderness in the past.

Not withstanding these stories, the possibility of being assaulted by a wolf is extremely remote. Instead of seeking people out, wolves will go out of their way to elude them. In addition, wolves prey on other animals only to satisfy their food requirements. They do not usually kill more than they need and they do not kill just for the sake of slaughter. In addition, wolves tend to select the sick, the weak or the old instead of the strongest, fittest, and youngest prey animals. By doing this, wolves play an important role in the ecosystem. By destroying the weak, they strengthen the overall population of their prey.

Their method of killing may also be more "humane" than folklore depicts. For example, David Mech, who lived with and studied wolves in the Arctic, observed wolves killing large animals such as musk ox first-hand, grabbing them first by the nose and then by the ear. In his book, *The Arctic Wolf*, Mech says studies on caribou and rats illustrate that taking these animals by the nose triggers a morphine-like substance that may tranquilize the animal during stress.

Aside from preying on animals such as deer and elk, wolves also prey on domestic animals such as cattle. This creates a conflict between those who wish to protect the wolf and others who fear the loss of their livestock. Wolves can also present a hazard to your dog. Wolves will destroy dogs, sending one wolf in to lure the dog away, and then moving in as a pack to fight and kill it. This happens especially when the dog is a female in heat. Wolves can also breed with wild dogs creating hybrid packs. Because of the potential wolf/dog conflict, keep your dog on a leash in the backcountry. You may also have to exercise caution if you live near wolf habitat.

One of the most significant conflicts between people and wolves occurs not in the backcountry but on the roadways. Wolves travel long distances and can use major highways as well as smaller roads. A collision may result in injury to a vehicle or the person driving it. It also poses a significant threat to the wolf. In some mountainous parks, vehicles are one of the largest causes of wolf mortality. Since wolves reproduce quite slowly and only small populations may exist in some mountainous areas, park officials advise visitors to obey posted speed limits. This helps protect both wolves and people.

TIPS FOR AVOIDING ENCOUNTERS WITH WOLVES

Mountain adventurers do not need to try to avoid wolves. Wolves will generally go great lengths to avoid people. However, keep your dog on a leash when in wolf habitat.

WOLVES
(continued)

Wolf Tracks

REFERENCES

Sources for this book include interviews with experts and survivors, reports from wardens, rangers, and others; the personal mountain search and rescue library of Lloyd Gallagher, and numerous books and articles. A few of the key publications include the following:

Daffern, Tony. *Avalanche Safety for Skiers & Climbers*. Calgary, Alberta: Rocky Mountain Books.

Gadd, B. 1995. *Handbook of the Canadian Rockies*. Jasper, Alberta: Corax Press.

Graydon, Don, ed. Mountaineering: *The Freedom of the Hills*. Fifth Edition. Seattle, Washington: The Mountaineers.

Herrero, S. *Bear Attacks: Their Causes and Avoidance*. Piscataway, N.J.: New Century, 1985.

Kershaw, L., MacKinnon, A., Pojar, J. *Plants of the Rocky Mountains*. Edmonton, Alberta: Lone Pine Publishing.

LaChapelle, Ed. *The ABC of Avalanche Safety*, Second Edition. Seattle, Washington: The Mountaineers.

Setnicka, Tim J. *Wilderness Search and Rescue*. Boston, MA. Appalachian Mountain Club.

Selters, Andy. *Glacier Travel and Crevasse Rescue*. Seattle, Washington: The Mountaineers.

Wilkerson, James A., ed. *Medicine for Mountaineering*. Seattle, Washington: The Mountaineers.

ACKNOWLEDGEMENTS

Although I researched and wrote this book, it does not represent the efforts of just one person. *Basic Mountain Safety From A to Z* was a team effort, made possible by the time and expertise of a number of people who are committed to mountain safety. In particular, I would like to give my heartfelt thanks to Lloyd Gallagher for inspiring me to rewrite the entire book with a focus on hazard identification and routefinding; David Poll for providing valuable research and reviews of the wildlife material; Terry Kenny for reviewing the medical aspects; Bruce Tremper for reviewing the entire avalanche section, and Robert Bott for providing editorial direction, advice, and support.

My thanks also go to the following people for their considerable technical advice and project support: George Field, Dave Hanna, Stephen Herrero, Charles Labatiuk, James Phipps, Margo Pybus, Ron Quaife, Freddie Snalam, and Terry Willis. I would also like to thank the rangers, wardens, and public safety officers of Canada's national and provincial mountain parks, who provided valuable direction and research. Staff of American mountain parks also gave generously of their time and expertise.

Finally, my thanks go to my friends Michelle Bastock, Kathy Besserer, Glenn Comfort, Alan Hobson, Susan Merriam, Patti Mayer, and Brian Strueby. Without their support, I could not have completed this book

INDEX

Index

J. Leslie Johnson

J. Leslie Johnson, a native of Alberta, Canada, was born and raised near the Canadian Rockies. She fell in love with the mountains more than 20 years ago and has been exploring them ever since.

Graduating with degrees in English and Classics, and 16 mm Film and Television, Johnson has written extensively about the Rocky Mountains. Her work includes several films, as well as television programs, slide/tape presentations and magazine articles. The subject matter ranges from landscape sculpturing by water erosion to a social history of Canada's first national park. Currently, Johnson works as a freelance writer and editor.

Among her other projects, Johnson is currently writing a book about birds of prey of the Rocky Mountains, and researching a book about the sacred aspect of the mountains.

Photographers

David Creith / Sahtu: 68, 90, 138-139

Marlene Ford / Sahtu: 15

James Frank: Front Cover, Back Cover

Alan Hobson: 40, courtesy Alan Hobson

J. Leslie Johnson: 4, 5, 9, 17, 24, 26, 32, 33a, 33b, 34, 35, 38, 43, 60, 61, 65, 72, 77, 101, 107, 114, 125, 126, 131, 137, 143, 151, 160

Bruce Kirkby: 7

Maria Neary: 21

Dennis Schmidt: 48, 55, 56, 93, 98, 99, 133

Esther Schmidt: 41, 42, 62, 79, 105, 111, 123, 144, 154

Freddie Snalam: 6, 18, 23, 36, 59, 75, 85, 108-109, 115, 117, 119, 121, 134, 136